The Manager's Pocket Guide to Effective Meetings

Steve Kaye, Ph.D.

HRD Press
Amherst, Massachusetts

Published by:

HRD Press
22 Amherst Road
Amherst, MA 01002
1-800-822-2801
  (U.S. and Canada)
1-413-253-3488
1-413-253-3490 (Fax)
www.hrdpress.com

ISBN 0-87425-449-3

Cover design by Eileen Klockars
Productions services by Steve Kaye
Editorial services by Suzanne Bay

 PRINTED IN CANADA

The Manager's Pocket Guide to
Effective Meetings

Contents

Introduction

Meetings – Business Quagmire or Valuable Activity?

Most executives believe that they spend too much time in meetings. They resent this, too, because they know the success of their business depends upon their leadership, not their endurance. They know that planning, coaching, communicating, and learning are essential leadership activities. And yet, meetings keep them from these tasks.

Quick Quiz

How much time do you spend in meetings?

None		Half			All
0%	20%	40%	60%	80%	100%

How productive are meetings that you attend?

☹		☺			☺
0%	20%	40%	60%	80%	100%

Results: If, for example, you spend 60% of your time in meetings that are 50% productive, you are

wasting 30% of your work time. Think of what
you could accomplish with that time.

Executive Summary - Here's What to Do

Tip 1
Prepare an agenda for your meetings. Without an
agenda you risk losing control and ending up
with no results. (Chapters 1 and 2)

Tip 2
Write a clear, complete description of the results
that you want to achieve by the end of the meeting. Then check to see if a meeting is the best
means of getting there. (Chapter 2)

Tip 3
Use structured activities (process tools) in your
meetings. These keep people focused on the
issues and make systematic progress toward
results. (Chapter 3)

Tip 4
Make sure that action items identified in the meeting include all the information that you need to
define the task and track its progress. (Chapter 4)

Tip 5
Model the behavior that you expect from others
in meetings. People imitate their leaders because
actions speak louder than rules. (Chapter 5)

Tip 6
Realize that amazing ideas lead to better ideas.
Design meetings that allow creative thinking
followed by critical analysis. (Chapter 6)

Tip 7
Include a facilitator to manage the process of
your meetings. If you choose to facilitate your
meeting, you remove yourself from participating
in the meeting. (Chapter 7)

Tip 8
Deal with unproductive behavior diplomatically.
This protects egos and creates a productive
environment that keeps people participating.
(Chapters 8 through 10)

Tip 9
Use video and audio conferences to save travel
time when meeting with people at other locations. This can give you a tremendous advantage
over competitors who spend their time sitting in
airports between meetings. (Chapters 11 and 12)

Tip 10
Set aside extra planning time when using high
tech tools to make sure you obtain full value from
them. Include information in your agenda that
describes how the tools will be used. That can
include instructions for technicians, camera
operators, and facilitators. (Chapters 11 and 12)

Tip 11

Understand that audio and videoconference meetings are often recorded. Thus, plan your statements carefully and speak clearly. (Chapters 11 and 12)

Tip 12

Use computers to supercharge the efficiency and effectiveness of meetings. They will speed up idea collection and results processing. (Chapter 14)

The Benefits of Reading This Book

The following chapters show you how you can distinguish yourself as an effective leader by holding meetings that produce results. That will help you and your business prosper.

Section 1

The Elements of an Effective Meeting

Leading a meeting is easy when you are prepared. The keys to preparation include setting clear goals, making realistic plans, and arranging for positive outcomes. The chapters in this section show you how to do that.

When you apply these techniques, your meetings will run smoothly. You will maintain control. And you will produce results—fast.

Effective meetings contribute to the advancement of your business and your career.

Best of success.

Chapter 1

When to Hold a Meeting

An Important Definition

Often, people call a meeting for activities that can be handled through other processes that are far more efficient. To avoid this mistake, compare your activity with the following definition. If it fails to match, your activity can be better accomplished in other less expensive ways.

Definition

> A meeting is a *team activity* where *select people* gather to *perform work* that requires *group effort.*

This definition contains key words that relate to the following important aspects of a meeting:

1. Team Activity

Meetings require teamwork to succeed. That means they are based on mutual support, shared effort, and common gain. Everyone works together for results that benefit the organization. There are no idols, no scapegoats, and no victims on a team. Instead, the participants cooperate with each other, coordinate their efforts, and concentrate on progress. Successful meetings embody the best of team effort.

2. Select People

Effective meetings include only those people who can make significant contributions to the process, which is usually less than a dozen. Marginal contributors, spectators, curiosity seekers, lost souls, and trouble makers should be left out. If they want to find out what happened, you can send them a copy of the minutes. (You do plan to publish minutes, don't you?)

There are special situations where a large number of people can effectively work together in a meeting. See Chapter 14 on Computer-Aided Meetings.

3. Perform Work

Meetings are a business activity where everyone works to earn a profit on the company's investment in their time. They are conducted with a sense of urgency. They are intense work. They are not an excuse to avoid the work waiting in the in-basket or to socialize in elegant conference rooms.

4. Group Effort

A meeting consists of activities that require a group to be connected together to produce results. Any task that can be performed by individuals should be left out or thrown out of a meeting.

When you plan an agenda, compare your meeting with the definition for an effective meeting. If it matches, you have a meeting. If it fails to match, you have something else, such as a party, an argument, a circus, a lecture, a convention, or a waste of time.

Does This Exclude Staff Meetings?

Many groups hold staff, "cross-feed," or information exchange meetings that seem to be exceptions to the above definition. In this case, the group gathers to discuss business, trade news, and receive direction. The key to obtaining value from these meetings is to make them into team activities.

Here are ways to make your staff meetings valuable.

- Keep news reports short. Give each team member one to two minutes to report headline news. Follow by one to three minutes of questions from the other team members. Goal: to inform team members of news.

- Ask each team member to present a challenge followed by everyone offering solutions. Goal: to involve team members in advancing each member's effectiveness.

- Include a brief seminar, conducted by a team member or by someone from another group. Goal: to educate the team on new technologies or work skills.

- Challenge the team to identify improvements for some aspect of the team's business. Goal: to advance the team's effectiveness.

- Use the techniques described in this book to develop plans, find solutions, and reach agreements. Goal: to work effectively as a team.

Each of these activities is characterized by the following:

- It leads to a result

- It has a short time limit, especially when each team member participates.

- It prevents a minority of participants from dominating the meeting.

Leave These Activities Out of a Meeting

1. Distribute Routine Information

Many groups spend considerable time listening to people dispense information. If you use meetings to report news, instructions, policies, or other routine information you may be wasting everyone's time, including your own. Although verbal reports appear to be easy, they often prove to be less effective (and efficient) than other communication methods.

➥ Better

Convey routine information with memos, faxes, or e-mail. Writing helps you organize your ideas for clear, accurate presentation. Then, the participants can read, save, and refer to the information as needed.

➡ **Exceptions:**

- Very short messages (lasting less than a minute), such as "Next year's budget is due Friday." Of course if you have many short messages, you should combine them into a single memo.

- Announcements that require a personal touch, such as a beloved founder's retirement. In general, these are messages that no one would want to receive in the mail.

- Celebrations that build loyalty, such as the news of an annual bonus for everyone. Individual awards are often best distributed in private.

- Special announcements where you want to respond to people's reactions, such as the announcement of a reorganization. Be prepared with explanations, assurances, and alternatives before convening a meeting to release such emotionally-loaded news.

- Tentative plans when you want ideas that may change your final decision. This provides a wonderful opportunity to lead by consensus. Recognize that people accept changes more readily after they have had an opportunity to comment on them, even if the plans remain unchanged after their comments. Use the techniques described in this book to make sure you gain full value from the meeting, and be prepared for emotional reactions to any controversial plans. Note that such a meeting will fail if you argue with the participants or demonstrate that you have no intention of responding to their comments.

2. Discipline People

Never call a meeting to discipline, embarrass, or coach a person. Savvy leaders know that public discipline can backfire horribly. The target person will focus on feelings of humiliation and resentment instead of on your corrective message. Some people will manipulate the situation to become a victim before a sympathetic audience, making you appear as a villain. Such sessions can become the tool of devious peers who manipulate the boss into punishing their enemies. And lastly, such a tactic communicates to everyone that you exercise mean, destructive behavior. That will destroy the trust you need to be an effective leader.

➡ Better
Conduct all coaching sessions in private.

➡ Exceptions
None. For example, a boss used staff meetings to correct and criticize the group's work progress. Such a meeting made a public display of everyone's errors. The result was that everyone resented this boss, which may explain why this boss was passed over for many promotions.

A true leader would have met privately with each person to resolve these issues.

3. Any Task That Can Be Completed by an Individual or Small Group

Meetings become inefficient when some of the participants have to watch a small group (or even worse, an individual) perform a task.

➡ **Better**

Plan meetings that include only those activities that require participation by the entire group. Any activity that can be performed by a sub-group should be assigned and completed before the meeting. Of course, some of these activities may require that the small group hold a meeting to resolve the issue. The key point is that they work on that task without making the rest of the group waste their time watching.

During a meeting, watch for tasks, activities, or decisions that can be assigned to an individual or small group. Then, mark these as action items as soon as you detect them and proceed with the rest of the meeting.

➡ **Exceptions**

A small group activity may belong in a meeting if it involves all of the participants.

- Small teams of two (best) or three partici-pants are more effective drafting text than an

entire group. If you are preparing a report,
mission statement, or any special document,
you can ask each team to draft the text or
write a different part of the text. Then compare or combine the different versions, ending up with a version that everyone likes.

- Increase individual participation by dividing
the participants into teams to brainstorm or
collect ideas. You can add an element of
competitive fun by offering a reward to the
team that collects the most ideas. Then the
teams can report on their results or combine
them into a larger list.

- Perform multiple tasks at the same time by
dividing the participants into teams, each
assigned with a different activity. Then each
team operates like a small meeting within
your meeting. Of course, each team is working on something that contributes to the goals
of your meeting.

Key Ideas

- A meeting is a team activity where select
people gather to perform work that requires
group effort.

- If your meeting fails to match this definition,
you have a different type of event.

- Avoid calling meetings to distribute routine
information, discipline staff, or perform tasks
that can be completed by smaller groups.

Chapter 2

How to Prepare an Agenda That Works

The Essential First Step

The lack of an agenda is the most common reason why meetings are ineffective. An agenda is essential because it focuses the participants' thoughts on the issues that you want to work on, and that keeps you in control of the meeting. If you want to distinguish yourself as a leader by conducting effective meetings, prepare an agenda.

A meeting without an agenda is like a journey without a map. Everyone spends a long time wandering about without ending up anywhere in particular.

How to Prepare an Agenda

Write it out.

Some people simply "think" their agenda. Then they play "I've got a secret" during the meeting. This is an effective ploy only if your intent is to bewilder, confound, and intimidate others.

Instead, maximize the productivity of your group by giving them a written agenda.

The benefits are:

- You can critically analyze and evaluate what you wrote

- You can confirm that these activities require a meeting and then decide who really needs to participate

- You can revise the agenda until it accurately represents what you want

- You can show it to others so they can suggest improvements

- You can send it to the participants before the meeting so they can prepare

Parts of an Agenda

A complete agenda has four parts and one activity. When planning an agenda, remember G O A L S. This stands for Goals, Outcomes, Activities, Logistics, and Strategy.

G = Goals

Goals are the results that you want from your meeting. They are the deliverables from the people in the meeting. They are the reason you called the meeting.

The first step when planning a meeting is to write out your goals for the meeting. Ideally, your goals should be so clear and complete that someone else could prepare the rest of the agenda and run the meeting based on what you wrote.

When planning goals, use the acronym SMART.

S = Specific. The goal states exactly what you want. For example, "Plan a job interview for the new sales position" is more specific than "Job candidate."

M = Measurable. The goal contains numbers, parameters, or some measurable item that tells when you have achieved it. For example, "Develop three strategies to increase sales by 5%" is better than "Boost sales."

A = Achievable. The goal must be a realistic achievement. For example, "Reduce production waste by 4%" is more realistic than "Eliminate pollution."

R = Relevant. The goal must relate to your business, mission, and work at hand. For example, "Plan next year's inventory" is more relevant than "My golf game."

T = Time. In general, the time component of a goal is the deadline. In a meeting this becomes the time allotted for working on that activity. You will specify this in the time line included in the list of activities. Of course, time can also be part of the issue that you are working on. For example, "Agree upon sales quotas for the first quarter" or "Identify ways to put Unit #5 back in service by Friday."

Realize that "ASAP," "immediately," or "in the near future" are not dates. People seldom complete goals written with such vague deadlines.

Examples of effective goals for meetings are:

- Identify three things we can do to reduce waste on Unit #5 in the next 15 minutes.

- Create a name for the new laptop computer in the next 20 minutes.

- Identify the causes of reduced sales in Region #3 in the next 30 minutes.

Once you have written the goals, ask yourself if a meeting is the best way to accomplish them. For example, if you want to distribute information, a memo, fax, email, or voice mail may prove more efficient. If you want to resolve a conflict, a personal visit may prove more effective.

Next, estimate the value of the results that you want from your meeting. Then compare that value with the cost of the meeting to achieve that result. If the value is negligible, cancel the meeting. If the process costs more than the result is worth, revise the process. After all, a meeting is a business activity and you want it to earn a profit.

O = Outcomes
Outcomes state the benefits of achieving the goals, indicating why you called the meeting. They can also describe the consequences of

maintaining the status quo. Outcomes are useful because they motivate people to find solutions.

They address:

What will happen? Examples: We will finish the year within our budget. We will keep our inventory up to date. We will stay in business.

How will people react? Examples: Our boss will congratulate us. Our competition will be stunned. The owner will smile.

What will we feel? Examples: We will feel proud of ourselves. We'll feel relieved. We will feel satisfied.

What will we see? Examples: We will see a shining new unit that works. We'll see our picture in the annual report. We will see an increase in pay.

What happens if we do nothing? Our market share will shrink. We'll have to reduce staff. Top management will assign this project to another team.

Use outcomes to sell interest in working on your goals.

A = Activities
The list of activities is the blueprint, recipe, or instructions for your meeting. It tells 1) what activities will occur, 2) who is responsible for each, and 3) the time allotted for each activity. For

example, some of the items in a list of activities would look like this:

9:00	Open meeting, review goals	Chair
9:02	Collect ideas to increase sales 10% in our division this year (Idea Harvest)	Facilitator
9:12	Discuss ideas (1 min. Balanced Dialogue)	Everyone

In total, this list should contain all the activities that you plan for the meeting. That means it should be so complete that you could give it to someone else and they could run your meeting without you.

When planning the list of activities, allocate time for each activity in proportion to the value of that activity. That is, plan your agenda the same way you plan the budget for a business venture. In both cases you want to earn a positive return on your investment.

A complete agenda appears later in this chapter.

L = Logistics

Logistics provide people with information they need to succeed in a meeting. This includes the location of the meeting (e.g., the room number and directions or a map if appropriate), what to bring (e.g., a laptop computer, data, copies of reports), and how to prepare (e.g., bring five ideas for increasing sales, write a draft of a report, survey your staff).

If you plan a meeting that will be attended by participants who travel from other locations, logistics can include information on lodging, restaurants, directions (maps), appropriate clothes, weather conditions, activities for family members, cultural guidelines, entertainment, public resources, and medical services.

S = Strategy

Preparing an agenda also involves extensive work before the meeting to make sure it runs smoothly, efficiently, and effectively. You (or an assistant) will need to:

- Meet with key participants to assess their support or opposition for issues on the agenda. If they express support, determine if their support is well founded. Otherwise, it could disappear when participants are confronted with more logical information. If they oppose issues, listen with the intent to understand rather than to change their views. Realize that if you turn these discussions into arguments, the opponents will refuse to meet with you. Instead, listen with acceptance, ask probing questions, and acknowledge different points of view. This research will give you the information that you need to find creative solutions or compromises in the meeting.

- Uncover obstacles to progress and resolve them before the meeting. This can include uncomfortable room conditions, inconvenient starting times, absent participants, missing materials, and faulty equipment. You may want to send an assistant to confirm that the logistical support for your meeting meets your expectations.

• Make sure presentations contribute to your meeting. Contact each presenter to explain what you expect from the presentation. If appropriate, have the person preview the presentation for you before the meeting. Also, insist that presenters rehearse their presentations with a clock to make sure they fit within your agenda.

• Check the emotional climate. Sometimes a major event leaves people too upset to focus on the issues. This includes events unrelated to your meeting, such as the resignation of a key executive or a reorganization. If that is the case, reschedule the meeting.

Sample Agenda

On the next page is an agenda for a meeting that starts at 9:00 a.m. Notice that it tells you everything that you need to know in order to prepare for and participate in this meeting.

Goal: To select actions that will increase sales by 10% next year.

Outcomes: A 10% increase in sales will exceed the CEO's goal for market expansion by 1%. This will permit manufacturing to operate at 96% of capacity, which leads to greater operating efficiency and related savings.

Logistics:

- Location: Conference Room A, Building 6
- Preparation: Bring at least three ideas for specific actions your department can take to increase sales.

Activities:

8:55	Arrive	Everyone
9:00	Open meeting, review goals	Chair
9:02	Collect ideas to increase sales by 10% in our division this year (Idea Harvest)	Facilitator
9:12	Discuss ideas (1 min. Balanced Dialogue)	Everyone
9:20	Identify highest impact ideas (Dot Vote)	Everyone
9:24	Outline action plan and assign responsibility for top idea	Everyone
9:28	Review results	Chair
9:30	Adjourn	Chair

This agenda contributes to an effective meeting.

- The goal for the meeting tells the participants what they are expected to accomplish. They can then focus their creativity on one deliverable: a plan to increase sales by 10%.

- The outcomes sell interest in accomplishing the goal. They describe how this result relates to the company's goals for next year and indicate the potential rewards for those who make it happen.

- The schedule of activities serves as a time budget for the meeting. It states how resources will be spent to obtain results. Of course, during the meeting you may choose to depart from this plan (just as you would with any budget).

- The list of activities tells the participants how they will work on each part of the meeting. That is, they will gather ideas with an idea harvest, discuss them with a balanced dialogue, and vote with dot voting. These process tools are described in the next chapter.

- The logistics ask the participants to perform work before the meeting. In some cases, developing a list of three actions could require extensive research, planning, and effort by the different department staffs.

- This agenda contains enough detail so that anyone can use it to lead the meeting.

- An arrival time is scheduled on the agenda. This gives people a buffer time to travel, arrive, and settle in before the meeting starts. It also provides a time for social interaction before starting the business of the meeting.

Tips

- If the meeting must last longer than an hour, schedule a break at least every hour. People need it. Otherwise they will think about their discomfort instead of your issues.

- Prepare the agenda with the help of key participants. They can identify the most important issues, select key participants, and plan activities.

- Tell the participants how to prepare for the meeting. For example, you could ask the participants to learn about the issues by reading documents, complete individual work by preparing estimates, or start innovation by collecting ideas.

- If you offer refreshments, make them available only during the arrival time. That separates the social activity of enjoying refreshments from the business of developing solutions. It also helps people focus on the issues in the meeting instead of on consuming food and beverages.

More Tips

- If you are the chairperson, ask the facilitator to prepare the agenda.

- If you are holding team meetings, let the team members take turns planning the agenda and serving as facilitator.

- When planning refreshments, choose foods and beverages that contribute to creative performance. Fruits, vegetables, and low-fat breads, for example, nourish people without putting them to sleep. Juice and tea are other options.

What to Do With an Agenda

Distribute the agenda to the participants far enough in advance of the meeting so they can prepare for the meeting. For example, if you estimate that preparation will require two days, then send out the agenda at least two to three days before the meeting.

Some people wait until the meeting starts before distributing their agenda. That results in an inefficient meeting because the participants have no time to research, study, or think about the issues. They also resent being asked to work on issues without adequate preparation.

Realize that unprepared participants will waste everyone's time preparing for the meeting *during* the meeting.

How to Guarantee a Bad Meeting

- Keep the purpose a secret

- Don't prepare an agenda, or

- Prepare an agenda consisting of a vague topics list, such as budget, overtime, employees, administration, sales

- Use the meeting to deliver a long rambling unprepared monologue

- Criticize, insult, and threaten the participants

- Don't let anyone else say anything

- Make sure the meeting lasts at least four hours, without breaks

Key Ideas

- The success of a meeting depends upon planning. An agenda communicates your plans to the participants and helps them focus on solutions to your issues.

- An agenda should contain Goals, Outcomes, Activities, and Logistics. Add an S for the strategies that ensure success and we have the acronym G O A L S.

- When planning goals, remember the acronym S M A R T. The best goals are Specific, Measurable, Achievable, and Relevant. In addition, they specify deadlines (Time).

- Include instructions in the agenda that tell the participants how to prepare for the meeting.

- Distribute the agenda before the meeting.

Chapter 3

Process Tools That Keep You in Control

Why Process Tools?

Suppose a football team played offense the way some people conduct meetings. They would show up without a game plan, without plays, and without a hope of winning. It might go like this.

Announcer: *"The Dingbats returned the opening kickoff to the 23-yard line and now their offense is on the field."*

Quarterback: *"Well, what do you want to do?"*

Center: *"I don't know. What do you want to do?"*

Left Tackle: *"Hey, you're the quarterback. You tell us what to do."*

Quarterback: Points to a player. *"Okay, you go out for a pass."*

Player: *"Where?"*

Quarterback: *"To the left."*

Right Guard: *"That won't work. He got intercepted last game."*

Player: *"I could go to the right."*

Right Guard: *"Does anyone have an idea makes sense?"*

Quarterback: *"Then how about . . . ."*

Referee: Tweeeeeet!!! *"Delay of game! Five yard penalty!"*

Quarterback: *"Let's just line up and see what happens."*

Announcer: *"Here's the hike and everyone runs in a different direction. The quarterback is sacked for an 8-yard loss. Wow, what a disaster!"*

Of course, no professional team would play this way. The difference is that professional teams use process tools called *plays*. Each play tells the players what to do and how to do it. These plays are designed to produce the predictable, reproducible result of advancing the ball.

Now wait a minute, you say. Last week my team lost. None of its plays produced anything close to a predictable, reproducible result. That may be true, and the reason your team lost is that there was another team on the field.

In business, you also have competition. And without process tools, your business has as much chance of advancing as the hapless Dingbats.

What Are Process Tools?

Process tools are structured activities for meetings. They are sequences of specific steps that produce predictable and reproducible results. They are also simple and easy to perform.

Process tools are powerful because they let people concentrate on solutions rather than the process leading to them. In meetings, these tools help people achieve rapid results through focused communication, thinking, and analysis. They also bind people into intellectual teams that accomplish more than any individual.

The idea harvest, balanced dialogue, and dot voting, which appeared in the example agenda in Chapter 3, are process tools. In the following paragraphs we will describe these tools and their applications in detail.

Applications

Use process tools any time you want a group to:

- Collect information
- Exchange information
- Develop solutions
- Find innovations
- Analyze situations
- Reach consensus

Process tools are so useful and so powerful that it is difficult to hold an effective meeting without them.

General Characteristics
Process tools make meetings effective because
they:

- Involve everyone

- Promote equitable participation

- Prevent anyone from dominating or avoiding
  the issues

- Make methodical progress toward results

- Facilitate agreements and consensus

- Convey that results were reached through a
  fair process

Process Tool #1: Idea Harvest

➡ When
Use this tool to gather ideas.

➡ What It Is
Everyone contributes ideas while a facilitator or
scribe writes them on chart pads. You can also
conduct an idea harvest where everyone types
ideas into their computers (See Chapter 14).

➡ Benefits
- This process tool equalizes participation. That
  prevents anyone from dominating the meeting. It also includes ideas from the quieter,
  more thoughtful members.

- It takes full advantage of the group's wisdom, creativity, experiences, and ideas.

➥ How It Works

1. Start by announcing the process. For example, you might say, *"Our goal is to develop a plan to improve customer service. We'll start with an idea harvest budgeted for 5 minutes."*

Tip

> Ask the group to suspend analysis, judgment, or questions during the idea harvest. These activities inhibit the open, creative thinking that you need to make this process a success.

2. Introduce the issue as a question. For example, you might say, *"How can we improve customer service?"* or *"What causes low yields on Unit #3?"*

Questions direct the participants' attention to working on the same issue. For example, if you ask, *"How can we reduce our budget?"* everyone will think about ways to reduce the budget.

If, however, you say, *"Let's talk about the budget,"* the participants might think you want to talk about:

- Ways to reduce the budget

- The inequity of arcane budget constraints

- Why their department deserves to be commended for managing finances.

Tips

> • Questions are powerful because they lead
>   people to think about solutions and they help
>   you (the chairperson) control the focus of the
>   meeting.
>
> • When preparing an agenda, plan specific
>   questions that lead to the results you want.

Give the participants a minute to make a list of
their answers to this question. Say, *"Take a minute
to jot down your answers to that question."* This lets
them build an inventory of ideas while you take
care of the next step.

Tip

> You can skip or shorten the time for this step if
> you asked the participants to prepare answers
> to the questions in your agenda before the
> meeting.

While the participants make their lists, write the
question on the top of a chart pad. This puts the
question in front of the group, where it serves as
a reminder of the issue.

Tip

> Save time by writing your questions on chart
> pages before the meeting. It helps to have an
> extra easel that contains the chart pages you
> prepared.

Then ask the group for ideas and write them on a chart pad. Print (best) or write clearly with large letters so everyone can easily see the ideas.

Tip

Write ideas in alternating colors to make them stand out from each other. I like to use green, blue, or purple. Black seems too somber, and red appears too dramatic.

There are important benefits to writing all of the ideas that the participants offer on chart paper. This step:

- Focuses attention on the issue
- Minimizes duplicate contributions
- Stimulates extending ("tailgating") and jumping ("springboarding") to new ideas
- Documents contributions for the minutes
- Makes people feel important and part of the process
- Acknowledges the first person to think of an idea
- Results in a more productive meeting

Encourage the participants to offer ideas by complementing their ideas (e.g., *"That's great!"* *"Wow!"* *"Keep going!"*) and stimulate thinking by asking questions that expand their thinking (e.g., *"What would please our customers?"* *"How would*

you want to be treated if you were a customer?" or
"What if you phoned with a complaint?") You may
want to prepare questions like these before the
meeting.

Realize that you will sort out the best ideas later.
During an idea harvest you want to encourage
divergent thinking. You want to collect a large
quantity of ideas. And you certainly want to
avoid any criticism or judgment. That's because
negative comments (e.g., *"That's a dumb idea!"*
"So, how would you do that?" or *"We already tried
that!"*) inhibit open, creative thinking.

When you fill a page, remove it from the pad and
tape it to the wall where everyone can see it. This
allows the participants to refer to the ideas on it
during the rest of the meeting.

Tips

- Prepare a supply of tape before the meeting
  by sticking two-inch pieces on each side of
  the chart pad frame. When you fill a chart
  page, you can quickly attach tape to the top
  corners of the page, tear it off, and stick it on
  the wall.

- If you are unable to use tape on the walls, you
  can attach chart papers to windows, molding,
  other easels, picture frames, or furniture. You
  can also use plastic chart paper that sticks to
  any surface.

Keep collecting ideas until your time limit ends or the group runs out of ideas. It helps to announce that the time for this activity is about to end. You might say, *"We have a minute left. What else can you think of?"* or *"I want two more ideas before we stop."*

Tip

> If you have a computer and a projector in the room, the scribe can type the ideas for display on a screen. (See Chapter 14 for more information on computer-aided meetings.)

3. Announce the end of the process and move on to the next step. It helps if you summarize the results. For example, you could say:

"That completes our idea harvest."

"We just collected 35 ideas to increase sales."

The person who conducts an idea harvest serves as a traffic controller for ideas. That person needs to guide and encourage the participants to maximize their ability to provide answers. As you might expect, facilitating an idea harvest is a full-time job.

If you want to offer ideas during an idea harvest, then you must ask someone else to facilitate the process. It is impossible to participate in this process and facilitate it. Attempting to serve in both capacities always ruins the process.

Different Types of Idea Harvests

You can change the results obtained from an idea
harvest by changing the way you collect the
information. Each of the following process tools
uses the techniques described above.

Issue Definition

Use this tool when you want to obtain a complete
answer to a question. Thus, you want to conduct
a process that collects accurate, realistic, viable
answers. To ensure high quality responses, you
may ask the participants to prepare answers to
your question before the meeting. And to make
sure you have found all of the possibilities, this
process will most likely proceed at a careful pace.

Your question will have a single focus. For example, you might ask: *"How can we increase our
customer base?"* or *"What obstacles hinder this
project?"* or *"What are the characteristics of an ideal
computer network?"* Notice that each of these
directs the participants along a single line of
thought.

Normally, you will end up with a relatively short
list of answers, amounting to perhaps a dozen or
two.

Brainstorm

This is also an idea harvest with a single question.
It differs in two important ways: the pace and the
quality of the answers. Use a brainstorm when
you want an innovation.

A brainstorm is conducted quickly with a high level of energy. You want to create an environment where people think quickly and spontaneously. You want people to suspend judgment, analytical thinking, and criticism. Instead you want people to adopt a childlike view of unlimited possibilities.

You should allow (and even encourage) truly absurd ideas. Often, the success of a brainstorm depends upon the extent to which the ideas depart from reality. This happens because radical ideas uncover new possibilities, which leads to creative solutions. They also irritate some people, which causes them to think of more practical ideas.

Thus, you want to create a mental stampede of amazingly radical ideas that stretches people's thinking into the unexpected. Of course, you will apply judgment later when you sort or analyze the ideas.

Tip

> Ask people to stand during a brainstorm. Physical activity stirs creative thinking.

Force Field Analysis
A force field analysis is an idea harvest with two dimensions (or questions). Use this when you want to explore opposing forces on an issue.

For example, a sales team may ask, 1) *"Why would customers buy our new product?"* and 2) *"Why would they reject it?"* The information they gather would help them plan a marketing campaign that emphasizes benefits and minimizes any detriments.

Or a project team may ask, 1) *"What are the advantages of a new system?"* and 2) *"What are the disadvantages?"* The information they gather would help them design a system that meets needs and avoids complaints.

Notice that the two questions examine the issue from two opposing sides.

Cause and Effect Diagram

A cause and effect diagram is an idea harvest with many dimensions. Use this when you want to determine the causes contributing to some effect.

For example, a quality team may ask, *"What causes 5% waste on Unit #3?"* Then they would collect their answers in four categories, such as People, Procedures, Equipment, and Materials. Of course, you can use any number of categories that relate to the effect you are studying.

The advantage of this approach is that it directs people's thinking into specific areas that contain solutions. It is almost like asking the same question in four (or more) ways. For example:

- How can our people contribute to this effect?

- How can our procedures contribute to this effect?

- How can our equipment contribute to this effect?

- How can our materials contribute to this effect?

When you use this process tool, it is useful to have a separate chart pad for each category. Some groups will collect answers on a fish bone diagram (see diagram) because this helps identify relationships between causes and sub-causes.

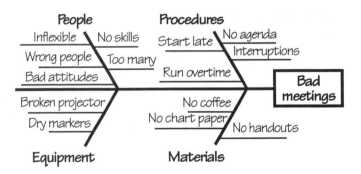

For example: A cause of bad meetings might be that people lack skills. Sub-causes might be that we hire unskilled workers and we fail to provide instruction.

This process can uncover complex explanations of the causes for an effect.

Process Tool #2: Balanced Dialogue

➡ When
Use this tool to control and manage discussion on an issue. This process tool is especially useful when you are working on controversial issues.

➡ What It Is
The participants take turns speaking for an equal length of time (or less).

➡ Benefits
- It prevents a minority from dominating the discussion. It also gives the quieter, more thoughtful members a chance to speak.

- It encourages people to prioritize their ideas and speak concisely.

- It limits the total amount of time that you will spend evaluating an issue.

- It creates a sense that the group applied a fair process to working on the issue.

➡ How It Works
1. Start by announcing the process and asking the group to choose (or agree upon) the time limit. For example, you might say, *"Now that we collected ideas for improving customer service, I'm sure you want to comment on them. We'll use a balanced dialogue where everyone receives two minutes. Is that okay?"*

Asking for agreement at the beginning checks to see if the group accepts the process. If it doesn't, you will want to determine the reason or select another process. Realize that a group will be reluctant or hostile if members feel they are being forced into an activity.

Ideally, the time limit should be short (e.g., two minutes or less). If the participants want to take more time than you planned, ask them to choose the time they will trade from another part of the agenda. Of course, if they choose less time than you planned, that leaves more time for other activities or contributes toward an early adjournment.

2. Give the participants a minute to organize their thoughts and plan what they will say. This important step makes the process more efficient.

Without this step people will plan their statements while others are talking. That destroys the intent of the process.

3. The participants take turns stating their views while everyone else listens. Each person receives an equal, maximum time limit. Usually the time limits are short (one to two minutes).

You will notice that most people finish early, speak concisely, and prioritize ideas. In addition, some people find it easier to listen to short pieces of information than long lectures.

When a group wants to discuss the issue further,

you can repeat the cycle, usually with a shorter time limit.

For this process to work, you will need a stop watch and firm enforcement. When a person's time ends, that's it. That person must stop, even if in the middle of a sentence.

The first time you use this activity, expect someone to challenge the rules. If you hold firm, however, you will find that the other participants strongly support you. It gives everyone a fair chance to participate and makes meetings go faster.

Process Tool #3: Voting

➥ When
Use this activity to select ideas for action or for further consideration.

➥ What It Is
Everyone votes on a list of ideas by selecting those ideas that meet a specific criteria.

➥ Benefits
- It quickly prioritizes a long list of ideas

- It involves everyone

- It can provide anonymity, thereby making it easier for participants to express unpopular views.

➥ How It Works

1. Start by announcing the process. For example, you might say, *"Now that we collected and discussed ideas for improving customer service, we'll select the ideas with the most impact."*

Notice that this example states the criteria for voting. Make sure you select a specific criteria that leads to the results you want. Vague criteria, such as *"best idea"* or *"the one you like"* produce mixed results.

2. Ask the participants to select a fraction of the ideas that meet your criteria. I recommend using a third, rounded to the nearest whole number. So, if you had 25 ideas, you would ask the group to select 8 ideas.

The participants can vote for their choices in a variety of ways. Select the one that best suits your needs.

- Dots: The participants place stick-on dots next to their choices on the chart paper. This method is dynamic and produces a visual result. In addition, you can use different colored dots for different criteria (e.g., red for highest impact, green for lowest cost)

- Checkmarks or initials: The participants write on the chart paper. This is easy because everyone has a pen and it avoids the expense of obtaining dots.

- Ballots: The participants mark ballots or

copies of the chart papers. This avoids moving about, which makes it a more practical approach in small conference rooms, and it offers the advantage of anonymity. Rather than have the participants wait, you might want to call a break while someone prepares the ballots.

3. After everyone finishes voting, tally the votes for each idea. The ideas with the most choices are the most popular. This produces a prioritized list of the ideas that best meet your criteria.

How to Prevent Discussions From Wasting Time

Many people use discussion as the primary process in meetings. Discussions require little preparation and use spontaneous conversation, which feels comfortable and familiar. Unfortunately, the lack of structure makes discussions inefficient. They often drift from the original issue, cover unrelated topics, fail to capture valuable ideas, favor a minority of aggressive participants, and suffer from the repetition of the same ideas.

➡ When
Use this activity when people want to talk about an issue.

➥ What It Is

Everyone engages in an unstructured conversation about an issue.

➥ How It Works

1. Start by announcing the process. For example, you might say, *"Let's discuss how we can improve customer service."*

2. Everyone talks about the issue.

3. You end the discussion.

You can improve the efficiency of a discussion by applying some structure. For example, you could:

- Set a time limit before you start by saying, *"We will discuss this for five minutes."*

- Present the topic as a question when you start the discussion.

- Ask a scribe to record the main points and agreements.

- Insist that people stick to the subject. If you allow someone to change the topic, you begin a new discussion.

- Alert the group before you reach the time limit. You could say, *"We have a minute left for this discussion. Let's bring it to a close."*

Why You Should Use Process Tools Revisited

These process tools focus the combined wisdom, experience, and knowledge of a group to obtain results. Indirectly, these tools also promote team-work, build self-esteem, and create success.

Make process tools the building blocks for the activities in your meeting when you plan the agenda. They provide a structure for thinking and communicating that helps you accomplish more in less time.

Tips

- Always evaluate whether the process tool is contributing to the result or hindering it. These tools are the means to the end, not the end itself. Thus, you should be flexible and willing to discard, alter, or invent tools as appropriate.

- Respect other people's ideas during all meeting activities. Realize that people produce more in a safe, supportive environment. Also, trust that the process will identify the best ideas.

- Let the participants decide (or at least agree upon) which tools you use. This promotes cooperation and represents true facilitation.

- Invent or adopt other process tools that meet your needs.

More Tips

- Team meetings become more efficient as the team members become familiar with process tools.

- In general, if you are the chairperson or the facilitator, make sure you stick to the topic. Introducing unrelated topics will distract everyone from the main issue.

- Use questions to guide the dialogue in a meeting. Questions identify direction, focus attention, and confirm agreement.

What's Next? Action Items

Once you identify the ideas that you want to implement, you want to convert them into action items. The next chapter tells you how.

Key Ideas

- Process tools are structured activities for meetings that produce predictable and reproducible results. They help you control the work in the meeting.

- Before using a new process tool, be sure to explain how it works and cite the benefits of using it.

Key Ideas, continued

- Use an idea harvest to collect ideas. Begin by stating the issue as a question, ask for ideas, and then write the ideas on a chart pad.

- Acknowledge all ideas offered during an idea harvest. This rewards participants, facilitates open thinking, and maintains focus on the issue.

- Use a balanced dialogue to evaluate ideas and express viewpoints. Everyone receives an equal length of time to speak on the issue.

- Select ideas with dot voting. Clearly state the selection criteria; then vote with dots, check marks, initials, or ballots.

- Discussions seldom lead to results. If the group wants to hold a discussion, maximize its productivity by presenting the topic as a question, setting a time limit, and making sure the members stick to the topic.

Chapter 4

Action Items That Lead to Results

Four Elements

The payoff in a meeting occurs when you convert ideas into action items. These are the tasks that everyone agrees to work on as a result of the meeting. At this point you should have reached consensus on the action items that you want to implement.

Unfortunately, in most meetings action items become lost and forgotten. This happens because the participants fail to clarify the scope of the action item or set directions for implementing it.

You can make sure your action items lead to accomplishments by answering the following four questions in your meeting:

- What is the task?

- Who is responsible for it?

- When will the task be completed?

- What resources will be used?

Ask the participants each of these questions and write their answers on a chart pad. This ensures

that everyone understands and agrees with the
direction you are taking.

Task

Even though everyone agreed upon the action
item, you should confirm and clarify that agreement. Sometimes you will need to convert an
abstract idea (e.g., reduce overtime in the shop)
into a specific action (e.g., hire two machinists).

Announce the action item and ask the group,

"Is this our next step?"

"Is this what we want to do?"

"It seems we chose <action item>. Is that right?"

If the group agrees, write that idea on the chart.
This identifies the idea as the task for the action
item.

Who

Then ask who will take responsibility for implementing the action item. For example, you could
ask:

"Who is the leader for <action item>?"

"Who's responsible for this <type of work>?"

"Who wants to do this?"

This may be an individual (for small projects) or
the leader of a department (for large ones). In
either case, you want to obtain the name of a

specific person whom you can talk to, instead of a group, (i.e., the Southwest Region). Write that person's name on the chart.

Completion Date

Next ask the group for a completion date.

"When do we need this?"

"When do you want to implement this?"

"When should this be finished?"

Depending upon the action item, you may receive a variety of answers to this question.

If you receive a specific date (e.g., *"tomorrow by noon"*), write it on the chart and gain agreement between the group and the person responsible for meeting that deadline.

If you receive a general completion date (e.g., *"by the end of next year"*), write it on the chart. Then ask the person responsible for implementing the action item to identify a specific date for a task related to starting the project.

You could ask,

"When is the first milestone?"

"When do you plan to develop a time line?"

"When do you expect to hold your first planning meeting?"

Write this date on the chart and gain agreement with the group.

This is a critically important step because it gives you a specific commitment that you can use to check on progress implementing the action item. When groups ignore this step, their action items become lost in conflicting assumptions and undefined expectations.

If appropriate, you may identify more than one milestone when you ask this question. That may be appropriate if the scope of the action item is large and the completion date is important.

For example, the complete answer to this question may be:

- Hold initial planning meeting next Monday
- Propose plan within 2 weeks
- Implement plan within a month
- Complete task within 4 months

Of course, vague responses like "as soon as possible" or "immediately" are not deadlines. Insist on specific dates.

Resources

Lastly, you want the group to agree upon the overall budget for the action item. Ask the group to estimate:

"How much do we want to spend on this?"

"What is our budget for this?"

"How big a <action item> do we want to build?"

This estimate should include the amount of labor, time, and money needed to complete the task. Write this information on the chart and gain agreement with these expenditures.

This step is important because it achieves consensus on the scope of the action item. The members of your group most likely had different visions of the action item when they selected it.

For example, a group decided to make a sign displaying its mission statement. The person who volunteered to make the sign estimated that it would take about eight hours to design the layout, buy a frame, and assemble the sign. But the group wanted the mission statement typed with a word processor and printed on ordinary paper—a task taking 10 minutes.

By spending a few minutes answering this question, we saved the company almost 8 hours of work time.

Examples of Action Items

Example #1
Situation: This involved a small task identified in a meeting between engineering and manufacturing supervisors.

What: Analyze the last quarter's production data from Unit 7 to identify causes of above-average downtime.

Who: Pat Smith (supervisor) and the process engineering team

When:

- Obtain data from manufacturing by tomorrow morning

- Analyze data and report conclusions by tomorrow afternoon

Resources: Four hours of work time

Example #2
Situation: This involved a major project identified in a corporate board meeting.

What: Design an ad campaign to promote the new Model 7

Who: Chris Wilson (Vice President) and the marketing division

When:

- Hold meetings with research, finance, and sales to plan strategies for the campaign, all complete within 2 weeks

- Draft proposed ad materials within 5 weeks

- Show proposal to executive board within 6 weeks

- Launch campaign within 3 months

Resources: $450,000 total budget

Leadership in Meetings

Successful meetings depend upon more than the use of process tools. They also depend on the existence of a culture within which people can work together for common gain. The next section shows you how to establish and maintain such a culture.

Key Ideas

- Define action items by answering four questions.

  - What is the task?

  - Who will be responsible for it?

  - When will the task be completed? (This can include key milestones, if appropriate.)

  - What resources (labor, time, and materials) will be used?

- Make sure the group agrees with all parts of the action item. Then document this in the minutes.

Section 2

Leadership in Meetings

True leadership is more than telling people what to do.

An effective leader works to create opportunities for others' success. They do this because they know that their success is derived from the success of others. The more success they create, the more successful they become.

As the leader of a meeting, you are responsible for more than making plans and using tools. You are also responsible for creating and maintaining a culture that supports optimum performance. The following chapters tell you how to create such an environment, even when other people seem to interfere.

Chapter 5

Leaders Create a Productive Environment

The Ideal Meeting

A productive meeting occurs in an environment where the participants feel free to explore new ideas, speak openly, and ask questions. They need to believe that their ideas are significant steps toward a successful outcome. They need to trust that all their contributions will be appreciated, including those that prove untenable.

This may sound like an impossible fantasy because real life is filled with tension, conflict, and adversity.

The key is the source of adversity. If it comes from outside in the form of looming competition, rampaging change, or impending bankruptcy, then it brings people together. If it comes from within your organization in the form of criticism, disrespect, or plagiarism, then it inhibits thinking.

As a leader, you want to make sure the governing forces move people toward your goals instead of away from them. The following actions will help you create a safe, productive environment.

Tell People They're Important

People contribute more when their ideas are appreciated. They think more freely when they feel important. They accept change more readily when they feel secure. As a facilitator, you can supercharge people's minds by appreciating their ideas. For example, you can open a meeting by saying:

"I believe all your ideas are important in making this meeting successful."

"I invited you to this meeting because I want to hear your ideas."

"Everyone here is an expert on some part of this issue and I need your help."

"Although we may have different views on this issue, I know we can find equitable solutions by working as a team."

These complimentary statements reassure people that you respect them and want to hear their ideas.

Set Ground Rules

Call them rules, laws, norms, instructions, or cultural expectations. They all serve the same purpose—to define a consistent, positive culture.

Meetings work better when everyone knows and follows the same set of rules.

The following ground rules are commonly used.

- Work as a team
- No rank (hierarchy) in the room
- One speaker at a time
- Be an active listener
- Focus on the issue
- Respect others
- Suspend judgment
- Allow curiosity, discovery
- Support others
- Participate freely when appropriate
- Maintain confidentiality

You may want to modify this list to suit the needs of your organization. If you do, be sure that you gain everyone's agreement on the new list.

Some facilitators begin a meeting by showing the ground rules and saying, *"These are the ground rules for our meeting. Do we agree to follow them?"*

Usually everyone replies, *"Yes."*

There is value in checking for agreement on the ground rules. For example, if someone were to say, *"No! I want to be rude and abusive, and insult people,"* then you can ask if the other participants support such behavior.

Ground rules also keep a meeting on track. If the group's behavior becomes unproductive, you can remind members, *"We agreed to follow these rules."*

Smile

This easy, inexpensive activity signals acceptance and confidence. Everyone can smile. The impact works wonders.

Of course, your smile must be genuine, relaxed, and friendly. We have all seen smiles that could freeze lava. Your smile should convey, *"This is a safe place."*

Actions Shout Your True Intentions

Most employees want to please their bosses. They do this by working hard to comply with requests. They also model the behavior that they believe will be appreciated or will produce positive results. This means that your staff will mirror your behavior.

For example, an executive I know was transferred to a new assignment in a large corporation. During his first staff meeting, he noticed several unproductive behaviors. Peers frequently derided each other's ideas, team members presented information with an abrasive know-it-all attitude, and some team members avoided participating in the discussions. These activities also occurred in the team's day-to-day activities.

With some investigation this executive learned that the team members were modeling the behavior of his predecessor. The previous manager had ridiculed new ideas, presented information arrogantly, and avoided controversial issues. The net result was a lack of communication that hindered productivity.

The new manager took three actions: He counseled individuals in private on positive approaches to communication, he affirmed the value of exploring new ideas in meetings, and he defended team members when their ideas were criticized. He also modeled the type of behavior that he expected. In a matter of days, meeting productivity and group interaction improved significantly.

As a leader, you have a tremendous influence over your organization. Negative, hostile leaders create hostility. Strong, confident leaders create confidence. Thus, make sure your actions support the type of environment that produces success.

The Real Test
Once you create a positive culture, you have to maintain it. In the next chapter we talk about real challenges that you can expect and will explore how to deal with them.

Key Ideas

- A safe environment helps people work at their creative best.

- You can create a safe (and productive) environment by affirming people's importance, setting ground rules, and acting pleasant.

- Your behavior speaks louder than anything you say. Make sure your actions support the environment that you want.

- Employees will imitate a leader's most notable characteristics. Thus, the behavior that you witness serves as a mirror of the culture your created.

Chapter 6

How to Deal With Amazing Ideas

Become a Cultural Environmentalist

People perform at their best in a safe environment. It helps them think clearly, make decisions, and communicate. That leads to efficient, effective meetings.

Unfortunately, some leaders create hostile environments that ruin meetings. Although they may advocate cooperation, teamwork, and integrity, their actions communicate different principles. For example, a leader may ask for creativity and then react negatively to new ideas. Such a response will make the participants cautious. They will avoid risks, seek safe answers, or remain silent. Then the meeting becomes a waste of time.

Thus, you want your responses to ideas in the meeting to support the positive environment that you need. As you must expect, some situations will make this especially challenging. You will hear ideas that bother you. If you are the facilitator, the group may challenge your role or make decisions that you dislike.

It may help to realize that you can accept something and still disagree with it. Acceptance means that we acknowledge without arguing, complaining, or fighting back.

It is important to create a safe environment outside of meetings, too, because your reputation always precedes you. Thus, the way you work with your staff can influence your effectiveness leading meetings with other groups. This is also important in team meetings because the same group of people attend every meeting. They remember what happened in previous meetings.

Here are strategies that turn difficult situations into peaceful victories.

Amazing Ideas That Can Be Ignored

Amazing ideas include anything that seems awful, bad, terrible, unfounded, impossible, stupid, dangerous, destructive, backward, progressive, shallow, thoughtless, insulting, unkind, unworkable, expensive, radical, unconventional, liberal, conservative, illegal, crazy, and original. Sometimes an idea sounds amazing because the other person thinks differently. Other times the idea truly is amazing.

If someone offers an amazing idea during an idea harvest, simply write the idea on the chart and continue. At this stage of a meeting, amazing ideas are relatively harmless because the participants will deal with them later.

Amazing ideas prove valuable because:

They stir the creativity of other participants, leading to better ideas.

They allow people to vent discontent, which then frees them to focus on solutions.

They allow people to test your leadership. If you accept a sacrificial wild idea, then they feel safe to share a truly novel (and valuable) idea.

Statements That Require a Response

If someone offers an amazing idea that requires a response, you have many options. Notice that all of these honor the person and then redirect the idea.

You can:

1. Acknowledge the idea and continue. For example, you could say:

"Thank you for that insight."

"I appreciate your remark."

"Thank you for that viewpoint."

After replying, look at someone else and wait for the next idea. This directs control away from the person who spoke and toward others in the meeting.

The unspoken words behind this approach are: *"I heard the comment and chose to ignore it."* If the disagreeable idea is important, someone else will keep it alive. Then you will have to exercise other approaches.

2. Acknowledge differences of opinion and invite discussion to understand and resolve these differences by saying:

"We seem to see this differently. Let's explore our differences."

"We seem to have different expectations. Let's talk further about this."

An open, candid response shows that you have the confidence and courage to rise above disagreements. In addition, sometimes a disagreeable idea is actually a warning, suggestion, or call for help. If you turn these situations into solutions, you will win respect from others.

3. Rephrase the idea in a positive way. To do this, first guess the rationale behind the idea and then build your response around that. For example:

Statement: *"That won't work!"*

Your response:

"You seem to want a different approach to our program."

"What do you expect would work?"

Statement: *"You ripped off the company with a fortune in stock options!"*

Your response:

"You're concerned about our company's compensation program."

"You seem to think I was unfairly compensated for my work on that project."

Notice that these replies maintain open, positive communication while retaining your dignity. In fact, dignified replies leave insulting behavior with the heckler.

Some insults are bait wrapped around a sharp hook. If you swallow the bait, you become caught in a devastating argument, which is what the heckler wants. Instead, move the conversation to a more productive issue where you can identify and fix the conflict.

4. Seek clarification. Here, you assume that additional information will help. So, you could say:

"Thank you. Now, how would we do that?"

"Interesting. Now, what would be the advantages of that?"

"Interesting. How did you determine that?"

5. Involve the other participants. Direct the issue to the group by asking questions, such as:

"How do you feel about this?" (This tests the group's reaction to the amazing idea.)

"How would this affect the rest of you?" (This explores the validity of the idea with those most affected by it.)

"Does anyone else share that view?" (This checks if others agree. Use this reply with caution because you want to avoid starting a popularity contest.)

"Okay, what do you want to do next?" (This asks the group for direction on the next step.)

6. Suggest another time to discuss the issue by saying:

"This is an important issue that we need to discuss. Rather than use our time today, I suggest we work on it tomorrow in my office at ten."

"That's a complex issue. I'll put it on the agenda for our next meeting."

"That sounds like a personal issue, which we should discuss in private. Let's meet in my office tomorrow at ten."

7. End the meeting. Some disagreements require solutions that exceed the scope, resources, or time available in a meeting. And some disagreements lose their energy when dealt with in private, without an audience. Thus the best approach may be to adjourn, deal with the issue, and hold another meeting.

Good News About Safe Environments

Safe environments encourage open examination of all ideas, including those that disturb you. Thus, other participants may defend you by finding flaws, stating objections, and offering counterproposals to amazing ideas.

Key Ideas

- Maintain a positive environment by rising above disagreeable ideas and activities.

- Realize that you can accept without agreeing.

- Amazing ideas often lead to useful ideas or disappear during later stages of the meeting.

- Deal with hostile comments by converting the issue into a positive statement that you can answer or by deferring the issue until a more appropriate time.

Chapter 7

Tips for Facilitators

An Important Difference

The facilitator serves a unique role in a meeting.
While the participants work to build solutions,
the facilitator works to build processes that lead
to solutions. This responsibility requires special
actions driven by a different perspective.

During a meeting the facilitator will use the
techniques described in this book. That is, the
facilitator will select and lead an appropriate
process (Chapters 3 and 4), maintain a productive
environment (Chapters 5 and 6), and correct
unproductive activities (Chapters 8 to 10). This
makes facilitation a full time job.

The Facilitator Manages Communication

Besides leading the group through the activities
in a meeting, the facilitator serves as a communication hub, by doing the following:

➥ Listening

The facilitator must fully understand what people
are saying, why they are saying it, and how they
feel about it. Although effective listening is a
topic in itself, the key is simply to pay attention.

Listen with every sense that you have. Listen with your ears for content, word choice, and voice tone; listen with your eyes for facial expressions, body language, and movement; and listen with your heart for feelings, motives, and warnings. Listen to what is expressed and to what is left out. Listen as completely as you can. Then use this information to guide the meeting process to maximize results, produce genuine agreements, and gather all ideas.

➥ Summarizing

The facilitator should frequently summarize key points made during the meeting. Such summaries provide mental milestones for the participants that show the progress they are making or the direction they are taking. It also helps them stay focused on their work.

You can summarize progress by saying,

"We have just decided to . . . ."

"We just completed . . . ."

Summarize feelings by saying,

"You must feel . . . ."

"That must make you . . . ."

You can summarize complex or controversial ideas by saying,

"Let me say what I think I heard."

"So, you're saying that . . . ."

These are powerful tools because they reflect back to the participants what they have accomplished or expressed. Possible reactions to summaries include:

- Agreement. They like the accomplishment and are ready to move on.

- Change. They realize that the result or direction is different from what they wanted.

- Retraction. A person reverses an idea.

- Understanding. All of the participants fully understand an idea after it has been restated.

Sometimes the facilitator will have to synthesize a summary based on incomplete information. This is useful because it challenges people with the implications of their ideas or the potential outcomes of their actions.

Active listening and effective summarizing require complete concentration. Thus, if you plan to facilitate your meeting, realize that this removes you from acting as a participant. It is impossible to serve as both a participant and a facilitator.

➡ Detachment

Sometimes you will feel an emotional investment in the meeting. You will want the best ideas and the people supporting them to succeed. Thus, you may feel tempted to participate in the processes.

When this temptation arises, your response should be absolute, complete, and total detachment.

You will be most effective as a facilitator when you:

- Stay out of the process (even if it seems like fun)

- Avoid taking sides (even if you favor one view)

- Speak diplomatically (even if people attack you)

- Communicate positively (even if everyone else is negative)

- Avoid fixing people (even if they appear to need it)

- Respect everyone (even if people express uncomfortable values)

- Act with courage (even if you feel fear)

- Remain calm (even if everyone else acts crazy)

➥ **Focus**

Facilitation requires absolute focus on the progress of the meeting. Evaluate each activity for its contribution to results by asking yourself:

- Is this contributing to accomplishing the meeting's goals?

- Are the participants working together?

- Is the use of time consistent with the value of the result?

- How is the energy level of the participants affecting the process?

- Are hidden agendas at work here?

- How do the participants feel about this?

- What must I do to keep the meeting focused, fair, and productive?

Valuable Tip

When someone is speaking, watch the other participants. Their reactions will reveal agreement or disagreement. That information will help you guide the meeting process to reach agreements.

Changing From Facilitator to Participant

I discourage facilitators from participating in a meeting. If you must, you should realize:

➡ Potentially Painful Consequences—Ouch!

- You risk losing control of the meeting. Without a facilitator, the meeting operates without a leader.

- You could lead the group to a different result than it would have found on its own. Then you share responsibility for the outcomes.

- You may become involved in an argument.

- You may add energy to a disagreement.

- You risk showing support for one viewpoint, which will destroy your credibility as a neutral facilitator.

- You may be unable to resume being the facilitator.

- Your contribution may alienate some of the participants, which will destroy your effectiveness as a facilitator.

- Someone else may take over as the facilitator.

➡ Potentially Positive Consequences—Good
- You may contribute valuable information.

➡ How to Do It
If you want to be a part-time participant:

1. Announce that you want to change roles by saying:

"I have an idea and want to participate. Is that okay?"

"I noticed something. Is it okay if I become a participant to tell you about it?"

If the participants decline your offer to participate, continue as facilitator. Caution: Forcing an idea on the group can destroy the meeting.

2. Acknowledge the group's approval of your participation. Say *"Thank you,"* and take a step to the side. This change in position signals that you changed roles.

3. Offer your idea clearly and concisely. Long-winded statements risk drawing you into full-time participation. If that happens, you fall into the negative consequences listed above.

Realize that if your idea is complex or controversial, you risk becoming deeply involved in the reactions to it.

4. Immediately return to the role of facilitator. Say *"That ends my contribution. Now I'm returning to the role of facilitator."*

Then step back to where you were standing because this physically signals that you have returned to your original role as facilitator.

Dealing With Unproductive Behavior
In some meetings, you may need to intervene to keep the process running smoothly and toward results. The next chapter shows you how to deal with unproductive behavior.

Key Ideas

- Facilitation is a full time job. It is impossible to be both a facilitator and a participant.

- A facilitator focuses on attending to the participants needs and managing the team activities necessary to produce results.

- Facilitators aid communication by listening and then summarizing the essence of what people said.

- Facilitators remain detached from the issues, personalities, and politics in a meeting. Attempts to become involved can destroy productivity.

Chapter 8

What to Do When Problems Appear

Expect Surprises

Despite your best efforts, some people will lapse into unproductive behavior. Left alone, this undermines everyone's productivity and makes it difficult to conduct the meeting.

When unproductive behavior occurs, be gentle, be polite, be firm.

Diplomacy Conveys Strength

I realize you may feel tempted to intervene with force. Direct confrontation such as admonitions (*"Don't be a jerk!"*), directions (*"Hey you, pay attention!"*), and insults (*"That's stupid!"*), seem efficient. Indirect hostility such as sarcasm (*"Here's another clever idea from the department with all the answers."*), trick questions (*"What kind of idiot would do that?"*), and indifference (*"Hummffff!"*) seem clever. After all, they work in sitcoms.

Such comments hurt the targeted person, create resentment, and reduce cooperation. They also

show the other participants that you can be mean.
That instills caution and ultimately reduces
everyone's productivity in your meeting.

In contrast, people find a courteous approach
more appealing and convincing. You will also
find it easier to apply.

A gentle approach is safer, too, because your
initial observations can be misleading. Often
additional facts exist that can change our perception of a situation. For example, in one workshop
a participant seemed to be sleeping during most
of my presentation. I wondered if the person was
unmotivated. Later I learned the person was ill
and had made a special effort to attend. If I had
lashed out with criticism I would have lost the
respect of everyone in the room.

When unproductive behavior occurs it is essential
that you maintain everyone's self-esteem while
restoring productivity. This keeps the person
causing it on your team and avoids a counterat-
tack, which can destroy a meeting. It also wins
respect from the other participants in the meeting.

General Approach

Use the following general steps to deal with
unproductive behavior in meetings. (Specific
responses to the most common disruptions follow
in Chapter 9.)

➡ Acknowledge the Situation

This seemingly obvious step is important because it brings the behavior into the open where you can deal with it. The alternative is to ignore the behavior, but this indirectly endorses it. And this guarantees that the behavior will continue.

In addition, people who ignore obvious problems look like inattentive fools. It's like having a bird sit on your head while you pretend that everything is normal. The group sees the bird and wonders if you know about it. When you acknowledge the situation, you end illusions that such behavior is normal and set the stage for the next step.

You can state the facts by saying:

"We have more than one conversation now."

"We seem to have drifted from our topic."

"We seem to disagree on this issue."

➡ Ask the group for help

A facilitator facilitates everything in a meeting, including the culture. Deal with unproductive behavior by talking to the group instead of to the source of the challenge. For example, look at the group and say:

"What do you want to work on next?"

"Could we have one conversation at a time?"

"How does this relate to the issue we're discussing?"

Statements like these use the leverage of group pressure to correct unproductive behavior. They also keep you above the nasty mechanics of enforcing rules.

Some people may wonder if these responses sound weak. On the contrary, they require courage. Even though many of these questions ask for answers that the facilitator may already know, their usefulness lies in letting the group select the answer. If the group selects an option that seems like a poor choice, then the facilitator should ask questions that explore the implications of that choice. Of course, the group's choice should prevail because, after all, it is their meeting.

Remember, it is far easier to let a group determine its culture than to impose one.

Next we'll consider specific responses to unproductive behavior.

Key Ideas

- Deal with difficult behavior diplomatically. Your perception of the situation may be incomplete or different from the other person's. And, in any case, you want to preserve everyone's self-esteem.

- There are two basic steps to correcting group behavior: 1) Acknowledge what is happening and 2) Ask the group for help.

Chapter 9

How to Stop Unproductive Behavior

An Important Limitation

The following sections show responses to the most common types of disruptive behavior. Of course, given the breadth of human creativity, other truly extraordinary situations may arise. For example, what do you do if the quiet manager on the third floor arrives wearing a chicken suit, throwing rotten eggs? Common sense suggests: call security and dodge the eggs. Your instincts and variations of the following responses will help you deal with the unexpected. And remember, as a last resort, you can always call a break or adjourn (see Chapter 10 for techniques that use a break to your advantage).

These responses bring most meetings back on track:

Situation: Multiple Conversations

This is the most common form of unproductive behavior. When someone begins a side conversation, at least two people leave the meeting—the talker and the listener. If allowed to continue, side conversations grow like weeds until they take over the meeting. Thus, you want to stop them as soon as they start.

➥ Response: Ask for Cooperation

The easiest approach is to ask the group for cooperation. Look at the middle of the group (instead of at the talker) and say:

"Excuse me. I'm having difficulty hearing what [contributing participant] is saying."

"There seems to be a great deal of interest for this issue. Could we have just one speaker at a time?"

"Excuse me. Could we have just one speaker?"

"Excuse me (pause to gain everyone's attention). *I know all of your ideas are important. So, please let's have one speaker at a time."*

"Excuse me (pause to gain everyone's attention). *Remember: we agreed to have one speaker at a time."* (Point at the ground rules.)

These statements acknowledge that a side conversation is occurring without naming the participants or putting them on the spot. You want to avoid hostile statements, such as:

"Hey! Do you want to share that with the rest of us?"

"If it's so funny, let's all hear it."

Indirect requests win cooperation and protect egos.

➥ Response: Use Process Tools

If side conversations continue after you ask for cooperation, you can adopt structured activities that make it more convenient to cooperate. For example, you could use a balanced dialogue or a speaking prop.

A speaking prop is an object that entitles the holder to speak. When the person finishes speaking, then the prop is passed on to the next person who wants to speak. Possible props include a gavel, paper cup, or any toy. If the participants are upset over the issue, select a soft object, such as a teddy bear or foam ball. It reduces stress and potential injury (if thrown).

Now, you say:

"We seem to have a lot of enthusiasm for this issue. So, let's decide that only the person holding the gavel (cup, teddy bear, foam ball) *may speak. Is that okay?"*

Notice that this statement begins with a positive acknowledgment of the situation (multiple conversations) followed by a suggestion, and ends with a request for cooperation.

A balanced dialogue controls participation by giving each person an equal, measured time to speak. Suggest using this process tool by saying:

"It seems everyone wants to talk about this issue. So let's make sure everyone has a chance to be heard by using a balanced dialogue. Is that okay?"

*"I think we need to use a balanced dialogue right
   now. Is that okay?"* (a more direct approach)

Is It Okay to Ask If It's Okay?

Some of you are probably thinking that the
question, *"Is that okay?"* sounds weak. Actually,
this is a powerful facilitation tool. It asks the
participants to accept a new process or a change
in the rules. Once you gain their acceptance, their
support follows. In addition, you can refer to
their decision if the new process starts to fail. For
example, the following statements will restore
order.

*"Excuse me, but we agreed to control our discussion
   with a speaking prop."*

*"Excuse me, but we agreed to use a balanced dialogue
   to express our views. I want one speaker at a time."*

If the participants reject your suggestion, then
you can offer alternatives or explore their reasons.
It is essential that the participants accept the
process you are using. When people are forced to
do something, they deliver minimal productivity.

Situation: Drifting From the Topic

New ideas are wonderful. You want to encourage
them, cultivate them, and capture them. During
an idea harvest, you want to collect as many
ideas as possible. You also know the group will
sort the diamonds from the pebbles later.

It's a challenge when new ideas appear during other parts of a meeting. They can destroy productivity by yanking the group's focus from topic to topic without letting it complete anything.

➥ Response: Question Relationship to Topic
When new ideas seem inappropriate, say:

"That's an interesting point (or question). And how does it relate to our topic?"

"Excuse me. We started talking about our budget and now we seem to be discussing payroll administration. Is this what we want to work on?"

"We seem to be working on a new issue. I'm sure this is important, and I wonder what you want to work on with the time we have left?"

These statements greet the ideas with compliments and requests for clarification. This recognizes that the other person could believe the idea relates to the topic, which it may.

➥ Response: Place in the Idea Bin
Use an Idea Bin to manage unrelated ideas. This powerful tool is simply a blank chart page posted on the wall with the title "Idea Bin." Some groups call it an Issue Bin or Parking Lot. The scribe writes new ideas on this chart or the participants write their ideas on Post-it™ Notes that they place on the page.

Direct new ideas to the Idea Bin by saying:

"That seems unrelated to our topic. May I put it in the Idea Bin?"

"That's a great idea. Could you put it in the Idea Bin?"

When you plan the agenda, leave time at the end of the meeting to check the Idea Bin. You will find that many of the new ideas were resolved during the meeting. If possible, deal with the remaining ideas that have merit or place them on future agendas.

An Idea Bin proves valuable because it saves ideas while maintaining focus on the current issue.

Tip

Keep a private Idea Bin. When you think of an unrelated idea (active minds have many of them), jot it down and save it until an appropriate time. That frees your thoughts to focus on the meeting.

Situation: Quiet Participants

There are many reasons why someone would be quiet. The person could:

• Favor a less aggressive behavior style

• Lack interest, knowledge, or commitment

- Assume that others are more qualified to offer contributions.

- Disagree with the approach being developed

- Feel intimidated

- Distrust the other participants or the process

- Feel sick or tired

Nevertheless, each person in a meeting is a potentially valuable resource. (That's why we invited them.) So, you want to maximize everyone's contributions in the meeting.

In addition, when participants hide behind disagreements, they limit their participation. This leads to false agreements, which waste everyone's time. Thus, you must uncover any hidden dissension so the group can resolve it.

➡ **Response: Encourage Participation**
When you notice a quiet participant, ask for contributions by looking at the person and saying:

"How do you feel about that, Chris?"

"What results do you expect from this, Pat?"

"Chris, how will this affect you?"

"Pat, how do you imagine this will work?"

"What concerns do you have?"

"How do you think we should proceed?"

Sometimes a quiet participant will test the environment with a tentative reply or a minor, safe point. Respond positively and with encouragement to any response that you receive. Then probe further to explore for more ideas.

Sometimes you can encourage quiet participants to contribute by making direct eye contact, pausing, and letting your expression say, "What do you think?"

➡ Response: Use a Process Tool
A balanced dialogue provides both quiet and dominant participants equal chances to speak.

Tip

> Different people have different views on what is too much. A quiet person may feel overbearing after making two statements in an hour. A dominant participant may feel left out after contributing only 95% of the ideas.

Situation: Dominant Participants
Dominant participants contribute significantly to the success of a meeting. They offer ideas, discover solutions, and make decisions. They can motivate others to take action.

They can also overwhelm, intimidate, and exclude others. They can rush people into adopting poor ideas. They can leave others feeling left out.

Thus, you want to control their energy without losing their support. Here are responses that help balance the contributions in a meeting.

➥ Response: Ask Others to Contribute
Asking quiet participants to contribute indirectly moderates the more dominant participants. Say:

"Before we continue, I want to hear from the rest of the group."

"This is great. And I wonder what else we could do." (Look at the quiet participants when you say this.)

"Who else has a thought on this?"

➥ Response: Use a Process Tool
A balanced dialogue equalizes contributions from all participants. You can also use sequential participation (a round robin) to collect ideas or control discussion.

➥ Response: Include Them in the Process
If you can't beat 'em, join 'em. In this case, ask them to help you with activities that support the meeting.

Some people want applause and recognition. So, you can trade private recognition for public applause. Meet with the person privately and say:

"I need your help with something. It's clear to me that you know a great deal about this issue and have

many good ideas. I also want to hear what other people in the meeting have to say. So, I wonder if you could hold back a little, to let others contribute."

"I can tell you're an expert in this area. And I wonder if you could help me reach other members in the group. I want them to ask questions and have a chance to discover ideas, just like you've been doing. So, I wonder if you could let them talk first."

Some people may want to lead your meeting. They think leading a meeting is fun (and it is). So, they attempt to take over by contributing tons of ideas on everything, including ideas about how to run the meeting.

If a participant tries to take over, you can retain control by giving away minor tasks. For example, such participants make excellent scribes. They can also distribute materials, run errands, deliver messages, post chart papers, run demonstration units, operate projectors, change overhead transparencies, act as greeters, and in general perform any logistical task related to the meeting.

This approach puts dominant participants in a controlled, prominent role while moderating their activity.

➡ **Response: Create Barriers**
Here, simply move away from the more aggressive participants and make less eye contact. If you are unable to see them, you are unable to recognize them as the next speaker.

Note that this approach could offend some dominant participants. Avoiding eye contact can imply disapproval, and sending such a message can change a potentially powerful ally into an adversary.

Thus, use this approach with moderation and support it with flattering requests for assistance, such as what has been described above.

➡ Response: One Point at a Time

Sometimes dominant participants will control a discussion by listing many points in a single statement. They cite every challenge, condition, and consideration known, which completely clogs everyone else's thinking. End this by asking the participants to state only one point at a time, after which someone else speaks. It is very difficult to monopolize a discussion when this technique prevails.

➡ Response: Preempt Comments

This is an aggressive technique that you can use once, perhaps twice, in a meeting. After that it takes on the subtlety of a club. It works best with people who have a sense of humor and a solid ego.

Just before the dominant participant begins to speak, acknowledge that the person probably has a valuable contribution and then quickly direct attention to someone else. This gives credit with one hand and takes away control with the other.

For example, while looking at others in the room, you could say:

"I'm sure [name of dominant participant] knows the answer, and I want to hear from someone else first."

"I'm sure [name] has already figured this out, and I wonder who else has an idea on what to do next."

"[name], you're probably way ahead of us on this, and I want to start over here first." (Point toward less-active participants.)

Notice that each of these statements starts by acknowledging the dominant person as knowledgeable, quick, or visionary. Be sure to speak with a pleasant, respectful voice. This will leave the dominant participant feeling complimented and willing to allow someone else to speak.

Tip

> Quiet participants often hope to be ignored; dominant participants want to be noticed. You will be most successful moderating dominant participants by building bridges between what they want and what you need.

Situation: Deadlocked Discussions

It happens easily. The process is heading smoothly toward resolution when someone raises a concern. Other participants join the concern.

Suddenly a gap appears in the agreement. Some want more data. Others want to continue. Now, the meeting is deadlocked.

Rather than become trapped in an endless argument, you could apply the following:

➡ Response: Form a Subcommittee

Ask for volunteers from the opposing viewpoints to form a subcommittee to resolve the issue. This is a useful approach, because:

- The issue may require extensive research, which is best done outside the meeting.

- The people who caused the dilemma will be responsible for solving it.

- The effort to resolve the issue will test its priority. That is, if no one wants to spend time finding a solution, then perhaps the issue (or at least the controversy) is unimportant.

Ask for a subcommittee by saying:

"There seem to be concerns about this issue. Rather than use everyone's time in the meeting, I want a subcommittee to resolve this and report back to us. Who wants to be on it?"

➡ Response: Ask for an Analysis

If only a few people obstruct resolution, ask them to analyze the issue and propose alternatives. You can say:

"You seem to view this issue differently. Could you help us understand your position by preparing an analysis of the issue with workable alternatives?"

As with a subcommittee, this approach will either uncover essential considerations or test commitment. In either case, it moves the deadlock out of the meeting so you can proceed.

If people agree to analyze the issue, treat this task like an action item. That is, define specifically what they will do, who will do it, when they plan to complete the task, and the resources (time) they plan to use. This is important because critics are often perfectionists who can take forever to complete a task. Thus, you want everyone's agreement on the amount of time they plan to spend on the analysis.

Some people are more focused on finding flaws than others. This is valuable if it leads to improvements, and it becomes a nuisance if it leads to chronic nitpicking.

An Important Reminder

These tactics apply only when the process in your meeting is deadlocked. Remember that meetings are an excellent medium for resolving differences, exploring disagreement, and achieving consensus. The different views of the participants are a valuable asset because they drive creativity to find solutions.

Situation: Filibuster

Sometimes, someone in a meeting will spin off on what seems like an endless monologue. You sit there waiting for the person's battery to run down. But on and on and on the person talks. You have two options: send out for food or intervene.

If you choose to intervene, there are two ways you can respond.

➥ Response: "Excuse Me"

Use the words *"Excuse me"* as a wedge to interrupt. It is important that you say *"Excuse me"* with polite sincerity. For example, you could say:

"Excuse me, I feel lost here. I wonder if you could summarize your key point."

"Excuse me, this seems interesting and I wonder where it's going."

"Excuse me, I'm sure this is very important and since we have only ten minutes left, I wonder if you could please tell us your main point."

I realize *"Excuse me"* can be a sardonic expression. Your tone of voice defines the difference between intervention and disdain. For example, if you say, *"Excuuuuuse meee,"* prepare for a hostile response. This approach works when you politely, sincerely, and simply say, *"Excuse me."*

➡ Response: Overlay Words

If the difficult behavior continues and you feel more aggressive, you can steal control from the speaker. In this case, cut into the monologue by repeating the person's last word or words and then rapidly continue with your idea. Although any words will do, this works best if you repeat the end of the speaker's sentence.

This is a verbal hit and run. Start by repeating the other person's words with slightly more emphasis than they were spoken, add a transition word, and then continue with your idea in a pleasant voice.

It is critically important that you speak with a light, playful sense of humor. You want to appear likable and almost innocent while you perform this dastardly antisocial act.

This sounds like a run-on sentence, such as:

"Huge fish-Right-and we're talking about ways to increase sales. Pat, do you have an idea on this?"

Note that the words *"fish," "Right,"* and *"and"* are run together as if they were a single word. More examples are:

"Pretzels-good-and we're working on our budget. What else can we do to cut costs?"

"Sloshed-wow-and we're selecting a new unit for the Western Region."

Tips

- Take a deep breath before you break in. Holding it for a moment will build the energy you need to race through your statement.

- This technique is most successful when the other person is talking about something unrelated to the business in the meeting. If the person is talking about a potentially related topic, you should ask the person to summarize the idea or post it in the Idea Bin.

- Look at the rest of the group while speaking.

- Use this with extreme moderation. If it's overdone, you will appear rude.

Situation: Personal Attacks

Personal attacks hurt people, mar communication, and end creativity. If they become part of a meeting's culture, they drive the participants into safe but perhaps useless contributions.

In addition, those who attack others steal control of the meeting. I once attended a meeting where one of the participants vented insults, obscenities, and sarcastic comments throughout the meeting. As a result, everyone sat quietly while this performer ruined the meeting.

I realize that you may feel reluctant to confront attackers. They often appear intimidating and larger than life. The best way to deal with them is to approach their behavior indirectly. You can:

➡ Response: Speak to the Group

Set the stage for the group to enforce its culture by making a general comment. Look at the middle of the group and say:

"We agreed to respect each other." (Point to the ground rules.)

"Just a moment. Let's pause here to calm down. I can tell we're upset about this. And we want to find a fair solution for everyone." (Take slow deep breaths and relax to model calming down.)

After making these statements, pause a moment to let the group respond. Often, someone else will support your request. Then continue as if everything were normal.

Important Tip

> Avoid looking at the attacker when speaking to the group. Making eye contact acknowledges and returns power to the attacker.

➡ Response: Explore the Cause

Sometimes people throw insults from behind a fence of presumed safety. They expect to avoid accountability. You can disrupt this illusion by speaking to the attacker. For example, you can say:

"Chris, you seem upset with that."

"Pat, you seem to disagree."

"You seem to have reservations about this."

I realize these statements may sound like naive responses to what the attacker said. However, such understated responses help improve the situation because they sound less threatening, feel easier to deliver, and preserve the other person's self-esteem. Realize that the attacker may have viewed the attack less seriously than it sounded.

After you speak, continue to look at the attacker and wait for the person to talk about what caused the attack.

If the attack continues, interrupt with:

"Excuse me. We need to respect each other. And I wonder what makes you feel upset over this."

"Excuse me. We heard that. Now, what makes you feel that way?"

"Excuse me. We agreed to respect each other. And I wonder what your concerns are."

➡ Response: Call a Break

If verbal approaches fail to end the attacks, then call a break or end the meeting. This will give you a chance to coach the attacker, rewrite the agenda, rebuild communication, and (if appropriate) schedule another meeting without the attacker.

➡ Response: Coach During a Break

If appropriate, you can coach the attacker. Remember: attempt coaching only when there is a realistic chance of a positive outcome.

If you decide to coach someone regarding a personal attack, you can say (in private):

"When you told Pat to 'Jump off a bridge,' I felt disappointed because that hurts the teamwork we need to finish this. I want you to express your disagreement diplomatically. Okay?"

Situation: Outbursts

An outburst occurs when someone snaps a mental rubber band. What follows is a volcanic eruption of words, anger, and fear.

The most remarkable aspect of an outburst is that the person who blew up may feel more surprised that it happened than anyone else in the meeting.

➡ Response: Interrupt

You must deal with this carefully and quickly. In a breath, you need to stop the behavior, acknowledge the person's feelings, and call a break (or end the meeting).

When an outburst occurs, say:

"Stop! I can tell you're upset. So, let's take a break to calm down."

There are three parts to this statement and each is essential. The word *"Stop!"* catches attention, like a splash of cold water. The sentence *"I can tell you're upset,"* shows that you understand the person's emotional message. And the last sentence *"So, let's take a break to calm down,"* leads everyone to a better place.

I realize that saying these words with the right emphasis may be a challenge.

First, form a time-out sign with your hands and shout, *"Stop!"* as if the word itself would stop a charging herd. Then speak the next sentence with reducing intensity, so you sound calm by the end. And finally, speak the last sentence with a soothing voice to model the emotional level that you want.

You may even find that the person who blew up will thank you afterwards for stopping the outburst and providing a chance for them to exit.

Whether you call a break or adjourn will depend upon the situation. If you call a break, you can resume work on the issue. This has the merit of showing that the outburst only delayed (instead of destroyed) progress.

On the other hand, if you adjourn, you give the participants more time to recover and repair communication. In most cases it will be better to adjourn.

➥ A Special Consideration

People with chronically low flash points may
benefit from professional counseling. They may
have learned to use outbursts to get their way or
they may have emotional challenges raging
inside them. Improving their behavior is beyond
the scope of this book and more than what you
should attempt. If appropriate, you could suggest
that the person seek assistance. (Caution: Suggest
this only if such matters are your responsibility
and if you feel absolutely confident that the other
person will be receptive.)

Tips

- Separate your feelings from the outburst.
  Avoid showing anger or attempting to over-
  power the other person. Most people instinc-
  tively respond to anger with more anger. That
  may have been useful in prehistoric times,
  but in a meeting it can produce a fight. If you
  interrupt, do so with strength, intensity, and
  deliberate calm.

- Some of the participants may have been
  especially disturbed by the outburst. If appropriate, you may want to meet with them to
  hear their concerns and assure them that
  work will continue on the issue.

Key Ideas

- End multiple conversations by asking for cooperation. For example, say: *"I'm having difficulty hearing our speaker. Could we have just one speaker at a time?"*

- Bring a group back to focus by placing unrelated ideas in an Idea Bin or by testing if the idea applies. For example, ask: *"How does this relate to our topic?"*

- Encourage quiet people by asking for their contributions or by using process tools that equalize participation.

- Discourage dominant people by directing your attention elsewhere. Also, ask them to let others contribute or involve them in the logistics of the meeting.

- End deadlocked discussions by asking the major proponents to resolve the issue outside of the meeting. Invite critics to prepare an analysis with alternatives.

- Interrupt a filibuster gently with *"Excuse me."* Then return to the issue.

- Counter personal attacks by asking the group for support or by uncovering the cause.

- Interrupt an outburst by saying: *"Stop! I can tell you're upset. And I think we should take a break to calm down."* Start forcefully and end with a calm, soothing voice.

Chapter 10

How to Save an Unmanageable Meeting

Two Trump Cards

You used the diplomatic techniques described in
Chapter 9 to end the unproductive behavior and
it continued. So, now what do you do?

There are two extreme responses that you can use
when a meeting becomes unmanageable. Of
course, these actions need to be used with discre-
tion. Otherwise, you create a new dilemma.

Action #1: End the Meeting

This is the ultimate trump card. Play it when you
reach an impasse by saying:

*"We seem to be stuck and the best thing we can do is
adjourn and finish later."*

*"We need to work on this outside the meeting. Let's
adjourn and continue later."*

A meeting is a vehicle. When it wrecks, leave it.

Of course, adjourning a meeting is like calling a
long break. The situation that made it necessary

to adjourn still exists. The work that you started remains unfinished. And the participants will wonder what happens next.

This means that you will most likely have to call another meeting to finish the meeting you adjourned. Use the time between these meetings to improve the situation. Heal your spirit, plan solutions, revise the agenda, and (if appropriate) meet privately with key participants.

Action #2: Call a Break

Some situations can be improved by temporarily detaching from them. That may be the case when you need time to calm down, silence to consider options, or privacy to coach someone.

Call a break by saying:

"We seem to be at an impasse and the best thing we can do now is take a break."

"We need to rest. Let's take a break."

Then use the break to improve the situation. You may want to:

➡ Restore Your Calm

Sometimes the events in a meeting will upset you. If you feel ready to scream, cry, run, or fight, use the break to regain your composure.

First, leave the meeting physically and mentally.

Find a private place such as your office, a stair-well, or the rest room. Take slow deep breaths, close your eyes, and relax. You may want to wash your face, take a walk, or climb stairs.

Then clear all thoughts about the meeting. Let your mind travel to a favorite memory or fill with nothing. Repeat positive affirmations, such as:

"I am okay."

"I can handle this."

Let yourself fill with energy. Put aside hurt feelings. Build a calm, solid, professional frame of mind before you return to the meeting. After you have restored your calm, consider solutions that put the meeting back on track after the break.

➡ Consider Solutions

If you called a break to escape from a dilemma, you will need a plan for dealing with it before you return. Find a quiet place where you can think and take a moment to relax. If appropriate, discuss your options with a trusted associate.

I recommend using private versions of the process tools to explore options. For example, you can conduct a personal brainstorm. Begin by writing a description of the dilemma as a question. For example, if you called a break because the meeting had zoomed out of control, you might write, *"How can I regain control of the meeting?"* If a disagreement blocked progress, you could write, *"What's keeping us from agreeing on this issue?"*

Then write answers to the question. Think openly, write quickly, and allow possibilities. When you finish, review the list to check if new options appear and select the most workable ideas.

Writing a list is a powerful way to find solutions. It helps you clarify the nature of the problem and collect possibilities.

You can also consider options with the help of other people. Just avoid starting a second meeting during the break. This can look like subterfuge to the rest of the group and make you late returning to the meeting.

➡ Meet Privately
You can use a break to talk privately with the person who seems to be obstructing progress. Before you begin, take a moment to plan your approach.

1. Decide what you want. Do you want information or cooperation? Then evaluate if a private meeting is the best way to achieve it. In some situations it may be more effective to facilitate a group solution in the meeting than to obtain one privately.

2. Plan the conversation. Put yourself in the other person's position and imagine how that person might react to your opening statements. When we feel upset, we may want to tie our message to a flaming dart. Your intent, however, is to improve relationships so you can restore productivity in your meeting.

You will succeed best when you listen empathically and assert gently (see important caution about assertions below). This helps you gain information, soothe feelings, build rapport, and ease fears.

3. Talk with the person. You can either ask for information that helps you understand the person's motives or you can coach the person on the type of behavior you want.

4. Ask for Information. Gain information with positive validations, such as:

"You seem to have a lot of experience with this system."

"I'm impressed by your energy for this issue."

"You seem to know a lot about the office in Region 6."

You can also ask friendly open-ended questions, such as:

"I wonder what happened the last time you installed one of these."

"What do you think causes people to feel that way?"

"How have members of your staff handled such orders in the past?"

And you can summarize your interpretation by saying,

"Let me tell you what I think I heard."

"So, what you mean is . . . ."

When finished, thank the person for talking with you, even if you dislike the information that you gained. It helps build rapport.

5. Plan how this information will help you lead the rest of the meeting. For example, you may want to:

- Suggest changing the agenda to apply a process tool that leads to solutions in this situation.

- Guide the discussion toward people who can add to, verify, explain, or refute the new information.

- Adjourn so major differences can be resolved.

➡ Coach the Person

Before you ask for cooperation, you must ask yourself the following important questions:

"Is this person's behavior my responsibility?" If the person reports to someone else, your comments could be perceived as meddling. In that case, you may prefer to discuss the matter with that person's boss, who is directly responsible for such coaching.

"Is a positive outcome possible?" Proceed only when your answer is an emphatic *yes*. This is especially important if the person holds a higher position in the organization than you. Attempting to coach a superior could produce disastrous career-changing results.

When you ask for cooperation, make sure that you send a positive message. This means that you must avoid accusations (*"Only a dope would do that."*), implied motives (*"Are you trying to ruin the meeting?"*), insults (*"Hey, nitwit!"*), threats (*"Shape up or ship out."*), trick questions (*"Just what do you think you're doing?"*), or verbal barbs (*"It should be easy for someone as smart as you to cooperate."*).

Cunning, clever, or cute messages always backfire because they trigger defensive reactions instead of cooperative participation.

In addition, it is very important to speak with a pleasant, neutral voice. If you convey even a hint of irritation, the other person will hear that more clearly than your words. That can start an argument instead of win cooperation.

Sometimes in my workshops someone will propose derisive feedback. When I suggest that positive statements are more effective, the person will say, *"But I'd want to be told that way."*

If insults helped people improve, we would have fixed all human problems long ago.

Use the following script to ask for cooperation:

"*When ....*" (state the facts)

"*That ....*" (state the consequences)

"*And, I feel ....*" (tell how you feel)

"*So, I want ....*" (tell what you want)

"*Is that okay?*" (ask for a commitment to change)

This entire message can be delivered with one or two breaths. It may sound like this:

"*When you arrive late it wastes our time, and I feel that this gets our meeting off to a bad start. So I want you to arrive on time. Is that okay?*"

"*When you call people names, this causes them to stop contributing and I feel this ruins the dialogue that we need to resolve this issue. So I want you to be polite. Is that okay?*"

"*When you carry on side conversations, that distracts other participants and I feel that this makes our meeting unproductive. So I want you to share your ideas with everyone. Is that okay?*"

Notice that these are clean statements. They simply state the facts, describe consequences, and ask for change.

Tips

- If you have time, write out your coaching message before you deliver it. This helps you choose the right words and eliminate hostility. Then rehearse the message, either with a trusted associate or silently to yourself. That will help you say exactly what you want to say the way you want to say it.

- Speak pleasantly with an even tone of voice. Requests for cooperation fail when spoken with sarcasm or screamed with rage.

- Recognize that unproductive behavior is often caused by a lack of either skills, knowledge, or incentive. Each cause requires a different type of corrective coaching.

Key Ideas

- If a meeting zooms out of control, you can adjourn or call a break.

- Use the time during a break to calm your feelings, plan solutions, or speak with the people causing the disruption.

- Request information and build rapport with positive validations and friendly questions.

- Offer coaching only if it can lead to a positive outcome.

Key Ideas, continued

- Coach privately with the script: *"When ...."* (state the facts), *"That ...."* (state the consequences), *"And I feel ...."* (tell how you feel), *"So, I want ...."* (tell what you want), *"Is that okay?"* (ask for a commitment to change).

Section 3

Telephones, Video, and Computers

Telephones, video systems, and computers can significantly enhance people's productivity in meetings. For example, groups at different locations can attend the same meeting without having to travel by using audio or videoconference systems. That saves some of the participants the cost and time of travel. When international or even cross-continent distances are involved, these savings can be huge.

It seems amazing that the most important executives in some companies will waste significant amounts of their time traveling to meetings. By using audio or videoconferences, they can direct more of their energy to the essential leadership activities that contribute to successful business.

Computers provide recording and analysis tools that let groups conduct surveys, analyze data, and share documents. That elevates the sophistication of the work accomplished in the meeting.

On the other hand, these meetings present special challenges. And when conducted without plans or structure, they can become less effective than the worst traditional meetings.

Here's how to make sure they work.

Chapter 11

Audioconference Meetings

What They Are

Participants at different locations conduct a meeting by phone. This saves people the time and cost of having to travel in order to attend a meeting. (See the next chapter for details on equipment for audioconferences.)

Audioconferences are appropriate for short meetings that can be held without visual interaction.

Possible applications include:

- Participants sit at their desks and communicate through a conference call. This allows a widely diverse group to meet without using special (and expensive) facilities.

- Groups of participants at different locations sit in audioconference rooms outfitted with microphones and speakers. This allows people to participate in a hybrid of a traditional meeting and a conference call.

  Most commonly, these meetings are held point-to-point (between two rooms). If more groups are connected, you may need to consult your phone company for assistance in setting up a multipoint connection.

- Combinations of the above two applications.

Applications

Sales Meetings

A team of four sales representatives meets every Monday to review sales targets, strategies, and news. Since each sales representative is in a different city, they conduct these meetings through a conference call. Each person is also expected to share a brief tip that will help the others sell more effectively. These meetings last fifteen minutes and serve to keep the team connected as a unified sales force that works together, thus maximizing their productivity.

An Executive Emergency

When an early morning fire destroyed Unit #3 at the Pittsburgh facility, the plant management had to act fast. At 9:00 a.m., they conducted an audio-conference with experts at the corporate office to review the situation and plan short-term corrections.

Top management was thus able take actions that minimized the impact of this disaster by the next day. Meanwhile, experts from the engineering department were able to identify the cause of the fire and make changes in the operation to prevent fires from occurring in the other two units.

Business Planning

The board of a major corporation voted to expand by introducing a new product line, stressing that the success of this venture depended upon rapid commercialization. The product had to surprise the marketplace to succeed. Otherwise, companies already established in that market would alter their products to undermine the competitive advantage of the new product.

Administrative assistants at the companies participating in this venture met by audioconference to plan a schedule of videoconferences for their bosses. In the course of these meetings, the assistants prepared agendas, planned logistics, and developed strategies for the meetings, recording their ideas on whiteboards. Within a week the plans were set for the first round of videoconferences.

Benefits of Audioconferences

The benefits of audioconferences include:

- Participants can meet without having to travel.

- These meetings are easy to set up.

- The equipment is relatively inexpensive.

- Team members can attend while traveling.

- Some (or all) of the participants can attend while sitting at their desks.

- Discussions can be easily recorded.

- Speaking into a microphone promotes more thoughtful discussions.

Special Considerations

Lack of visual contact creates special challenges for these meetings. For example:

- Audioconferences can degenerate into frustrating struggles with uncontrolled babble. This occurs because the participants lack visual contact with each other.

- When individuals sit in the privacy of their offices, they can lapse into unproductive behaviors like reading their mail or pressing the mute button to talk to a visitor. Such activities detract from the meeting because the other participants think everyone is paying attention.

- Participants are unable to see facial expressions and body language. These subtle yet important parts of communication are lost because the participants communicate only by sound.

- Participants are unable to see visual aids, demonstrations, or notes written on a chart pad.

- The success of the meeting depends upon having the supporting equipment set up and working properly. Normally, a technician takes care of this before the meeting. Equipment problems, though rare, can end the meeting.

- If an audioconference meeting is held in a large room, it can be difficult for those at other sites to hear everyone.

- Sometimes the system can produce distractions such as distorted sound, static, or reduced sound quality.

What to Do

Here is how to make your meeting effective:

- Keep the size of the group as small as possible. It is unlikely that more than eight people can effectively participate in a conference call. Small groups are also more manageable for point-to-point audioconference meetings.

- Plan short meetings, especially if the meeting is held as a conference call. Most people can concentrate effectively for about half an hour. Any conference call lasting more than that is probably a waste of people's time.

- If you must invite people who have minor roles, such as to observe or to be available as a resource, let them attend as spectators. If you are meeting in conference rooms, announce their presence at the beginning and seat them in less prominent locations.

- If you are conducting the meeting as a conference call, ask the minor contributors to work
  near their phones during the meeting. Then
  call them into the meeting only when needed.

- Plan meetings that deal with clearly defined
  issues. Use a balanced dialogue as much as
  possible. If you must hold a discussion, set a
  time limit and appoint a moderator who is
  responsible for enforcing it.

- Send copies of the agenda materials to the
  participants before the meeting.

- You can use visual aids if they are made
  available to all participants. Send copies of
  the materials (such as slides or overhead
  transparencies) by mail, fax, or e-mail to each
  group participating in the meeting. Then,
  during the meeting, tell the participants
  which exhibit applies (*"Next chart."* or *"Go to
  slide number 12."*). The remote groups can
  show that slide on their projectors, view a
  paper copy, or display that image on their
  computers.

- Begin the meeting with self-introductions.
  This helps everyone relate names to voices.

- Announce your name each time you speak,
  unless your voice is distinctly different from
  everyone else in the meeting.

- If you are speaking on your desk phone, use
  the handset instead of the speakerphone. A

speakerphone, while useful, distorts your voice, picks up background sounds (like office equipment), and makes a poor impression on the listener. If you must have both hands free while you talk, obtain a headset. (Note: It is more courteous to speak to people through the handset on all phone calls.)

- If you are meeting in teleconference rooms, have a facilitator in each room recording ideas on one of the following tools:

Electronic whiteboard
This is the electronic equivalent of a chart pad. Some models can be connected to computers, so that ideas written on one board are displayed in the other meeting rooms. Other models will print the information written on the board. Then you can fax this to the groups at the other locations.

Computer terminal
The facilitator types ideas on a computer, which then distributes them to all participants through an intranet or with the Internet.

Note pad and a fax machine
The facilitator writes ideas on a note pad and periodically sends copies to the participants by fax.

These tools serve the same purpose as a chart pad in a traditional meeting. They help you

record and display ideas before the participants. That avoids duplicate statements,
promotes more efficient discussion, and
captures information accurately.

- Speak clearly to make sure you are understood. Take the extra effort to enunciate
  carefully and speak slowly. Of course, you
  want to sound natural rather than overdoing
  this.

- When stating numbers, write them out while
  you speak because that defines the rate at
  which everyone else is receiving them.

- If appropriate, ask the receiving party to
  confirm numbers (or other critical data) by
  repeating them. Although this may feel
  awkward, it prevents misunderstandings.

- If possible, plan your statements by jotting
  down an outline of your key ideas before
  speaking. This contributes to a more efficient
  meeting and avoids the embarrassment of
  recording a verbal gaff.

- Use your best, most focused listening skills.
  In addition to content, pay attention to inflec-
  tions, voice tone, word selection, emphasis,
  assumed intentions, and your intuition.

- Enforce the rule of "one speaker at a time."
  Multiple conversations ruin a teleconference.

- Insist that people announce when they join or
  leave the conference.

- If people must leave during the meeting, gain closure on any issues that they participated in before they leave. For example, *"Pat agreed to prepare a cost estimate by next Monday. Is that correct, Pat?"* Make adjustments in the agenda (if appropriate) based on the remaining participants.

- Avoid using the mute feature because it excludes other parties. Also, some groups have experienced disasters by inadvertently transmitting private information when the mute feature malfunctioned. Call a break if you must meet privately with the participants at your location.

- If one of the groups is using a large room, you may need to provide individual microphones for the participants. This will ensure that everyone in the room is heard with equal clarity by participants at the other sites. You can also move a microphone to the person who is speaking.

- Avoid shuffling papers or tapping objects near the microphone. Everyone else will hear the noise.

- Prepare minutes soon after the meeting. Send a draft to key participants to confirm that your notes accurately describe the results of the meeting.

Key Ideas

- Audioconferences offer the advantage of bringing people together without the cost of travel.

- Plan audioconferences only for meetings that can be conducted without visual aids.

- Appoint a facilitator to manage the process and provide some means of recording ideas.

- Apply your best communication and listening skills to compensate for the lack of visual contact with other participants.

Chapter 12

Videoconference Meetings

What They Are

Videoconferences let you meet with people at different locations without having to travel. That results in significant savings in time and money.

Videoconferences can be conducted as either conventional meetings between two or more groups of people in conference rooms or as video-supported telephone calls involving individuals in their offices. Both situations bring people together without the expense of travel.

In a conventional meeting, groups of participants sit in separate rooms, each equipped with video cameras and monitors. Each group speaks in front of the video camera in their room and views the other groups on TV monitors. Other equipment in the rooms may include electronic whiteboards, fax machines, computers, and other video display equipment. The next chapter describes equipment considerations for videoconferences.

With a video-supported phone call, individuals communicate through their desktop computers.

A small, simple video camera captures the participant's image and feeds it to the computer, which sends the image to the other participants. These cameras cost about $200 and mount on the monitor. Images appear on the other participants' screens in a small (about 1.5 by 2 inches) window. The participants may speak into a microphone connected to the computer or through the phone system. Depending upon the software, they may also write text messages or draw pictures that appear in a windows on the screen. Video and audio quality are generally poor, with fuzzy images and jerky motion.

Two products are worth mentioning.

CU-SeeMe is a free videoconferencing program (under copyright of Cornell University and its collaborators) that runs on Macintosh or Windows computers. A newer version with more features is sold by White Pine Software (http://www.wpine.com). Transmission occurs through the Internet. With CU-SeeMe, you can connect up to twelve sites (eight sites with the free version). Obtain the free copy of CU-SeeMe from their web site (http://cu-seeme.cornell.edu)

NetMeeting by Microsoft supports point-to-point (two parties) videoconferencing and multipoint collaboration on files created with Windows applications, such as Excel or Word. Unlimited participants can also write text (chat window) or draw pictures (whiteboard). As of this writing,

NetMeeting runs only on computers with Windows 95 or Windows NT 4.0. NetMeeting is available for free from Microsoft's web site (http://www.microsoft.com/netmeeting).

Applications

➡ **New International Product**

Executives at a company in Los Angeles use videoconferences to launch new products in record time. First, they hold a series of videoconferences with executives in Singapore to plan the manufacturing strategy for the internal assembly. In these meetings they review proposals presented by engineers at both companies, develop scale-up schedules, and project market response. Then these executives hold videoconferences with executives at their plants in Houston and Dublin, as well as with contractor firms in Tokyo, Berlin, and Warsaw, to review and agree upon different case designs for each major market. Various designs are compared and evaluated.

Next, the selections are shown to the executives in Singapore to confirm compatibility with the main assembly. Finally, the company's marketing executives hold videoconferences with executives at advertising companies in New York, Tokyo, London, and Moscow to plan promotional campaigns. These executives and their staffs design advertisements and develop marketing strategies.

The new product reached the market in record time, offering features that significantly surpassed the competition, thanks to a rapidly implemented campaign of customized design, timely manufacturing, and focused marketing.

The key to rapid and successful development of such a complex project was videoconferencing. It enabled key executives from offices all over the world to conduct a large number of meetings in a very short time. On some days, executives in Los Angeles held a morning meeting (Los Angeles time) with partners in Europe, and then met with partners in Asia that afternoon. This would have been impossible if they had to travel to those locations.

➥ Software Development

Engineers in Dallas and Bombay jointly develop software via videoconference. Thanks to videoconferencing, the engineers work together as if they were in the same office, planning features, exchanging files, and testing code. Most of these meetings occur as brief, informal video-supported phone calls. Here, videoconferencing expands the company's human resources to produce products.

➥ Announcement from the CEO

A major corporation has decided to merge with

another company. The CEO conveys this news to all employees through a videoconference broadcast by satellite. Employees worldwide hear about the merger at the same time that the company distributes a press release to the media. Microphones at each location allow employees to ask questions and make comments. The CEO uses this opportunity to talk about how the merger supports the company's vision for expansion and to assure the employees that their future is secure.

By communicating this sensitive information to the employees through a videoconference, the company made sure that everyone heard an accurate description of the news at the same time. In addition, employees heard the news directly from the CEO, instead of hearing an interpretation from media reports. The system also gave the employees a chance to ask questions and express their views, which helped them feel connected with the company's leadership.

Benefits of Videoconferences

The benefits of videoconferences include:

- They allow groups at different locations to meet face-to-face without having to travel. People can give presentations, demonstrate equipment, and show things such as blueprints, photos, and products from different locations.

- These meetings offer significant savings and productivity gains for executives. They make it easier to stay in touch with co-workers, team members, and partners in distant locations, which facilitates the communication necessary for successful leadership.

- They can be used to distribute information on new procedures, technologies, and work skills.

- People are comfortable watching TV and thus pay more attention to the person on the monitor. Speaking before a camera promotes more focused and thoughtful discussions. The technical complexity of such meetings causes people to plan more extensively.

- Most videoconferences follow rigid time control, which helps maintain disciplined efficiency.

- You can easily record the meeting, which can help the person who prepares the minutes.

Special Considerations

As you might expect, the complexity of the support equipment presents challenges.

- Videoconference meetings require a complex, expensive system of video equipment and fast telephone connections at each location. Your meetings may also require other equipment such as electronic whiteboards, computers, fax machines, and video projectors.

- Technicians are required to set up, operate, and maintain the system.

- Some people find that speaking through a video connection is artificial and inhibiting. Thus, they will act more cautious during such meetings. That can be good if it adds to their focus in the meeting. It becomes a difficulty when it prevents candid discussion of the issues.

- Videoconferences will capture, record, and broadcast unproductive behaviors. This includes secrets whispered to the person next to you.

- Bright lights (if used) can reduce comfort. Theatrical considerations add complications.

What to Do

Here is how to make your meeting effective.

- Because of the expenses involved in setting up and holding of video conference meetings, it is essential that you prepare adequately. Your agenda, for example, may even include directions for the video crews at all locations.

- Send copies of the agenda and all related materials to the participants and support staff before the meeting.

- Before using new equipment, conduct a trial run to make sure everyone understands how it works.

- Arrive early enough before the meeting starts to review strategies with the participants at your site and become familiar with the equipment. Arriving late disrupts the meeting and makes a bad impression on the participants at the other locations. (Of course, arriving early is always good etiquette.)

- Use structured activities, because these help you control the meeting, record results, and make progress.

- Use an electronic whiteboard at each location instead of a chart pad to record ideas. If that is unavailable, use a chart pad that is displayed on a separate camera/video link. You can also record notes in a chat session through your intranet or on the Internet. These notes can then be displayed on a monitor or projected on a screen.

- If you are giving a presentation, rehearse it in front of a video camera. Then review the recording to make sure your actions and your presentation create the impact you want. If the presentation is sufficiently important, you may want to consult an expert on speaking in front of cameras.

- The cost of these meetings and room reservation schedules make effective time management critically important. Allow extra time for unexpected activities. For example, plan all presentations so that they end three to five minutes early. Also, rehearse presentations with a clock to make sure that they conclude within the time allotted.

- Face the camera when speaking because it gives your audience (the people watching you on the TV monitors) the impression that you are talking to them. Also, recognize that your audience will compare your speaking delivery with that used by professional broadcasters. Thus, minimize your movements, use small changes in facial expression, and make small gestures. Large movements appear flamboyant when displayed on TV.

- Speak clearly, concisely, and naturally. People are used to getting short bits of information from television.

- Take the extra effort to enunciate clearly. You want to make sure people understand what you say.

- Use visual aids to support presentations of data, complex ideas, or critical information. This enhances the impact and increases your chances of being understood.

- Model your delivery of key points after television commercials. That is, plan simple, focused descriptions that last a minute or less.

- Avoid shuffling papers or tapping objects near the microphone. Everyone else will hear the noise.

Types of Video Systems

When selecting video cameras, you have four basic choices.

➡ Fixed Camera

All of the participants face one camera that is mounted on a tripod. This is the least expensive and least complex option. If you use this system, plan for small groups of people at each location. It is difficult to see the faces and facial expressions of more than four people on a monitor.

➡ Voice-activated Camera

The video camera is mounted on a mechanism that points the lens at the source of sound. Generally, the camera is focused to fill the screen with a person's image, as on a commercial news broadcast. If you use this option, it is essential that everyone else remain silent when someone speaks. If you have individual microphones, you may want to turn off your microphone when you finish speaking.

➡ Remote-Controlled Camera

The video camera is mounted on a mechanism that points the lens as directed by control buttons.

➦ Camera Operator
This provides the best control and most flexibility managing the video camera. Of course, you incur the costs of a camera operator.

What to Wear
Your appearance on camera can be different from what you expect. Support lighting and camera resolution can exaggerate or distort the impact of trendy outfits, producing undesirable results. Here are suggestions on how to look your best:

• Wear solid colors. Plaids and small patterns can appear fuzzy on camera. Instead, select a jacket or suit in a solid, medium-to-dark color.

• Avoid white and bright red. Some cameras have difficulty capturing these colors. Instead of white, wear light blue or pastel colors.

• Avoid sheer or tight clothes because under some lighting situations these can appear revealing or unflattering.

• Avoid large jewelry because it can cause glaring reflections. Jewelry may be acceptable under soft ambient lighting.

• Avoid shiny fabrics because these can produce glare.

• Wear light makeup because it makes you appear healthy. Heavy makeup will make you look older and no makeup can leave you appearing pale. Makeup will also prevent support lighting from reflecting off your face.

Key Ideas

- Videoconferences offer the advantage of bringing people together without the cost of travel.

- Extensive planning is necessary to make sure the meeting makes full use of this expensive resource and fits in with tight schedules.

- Model your speaking after commercial television announcers. Face the camera, speak clearly, make concise points.

- If you are giving a presentation, rehearse before a camera and use a clock. Then review your presentation to make sure you create the impression you want.

- Select clothing that appears attractive on television.

Chapter 13

Videoconference Equipment

Videoconference equipment is complex and based on rapidly evolving technologies. A complete description of all the information and resources for these systems would fill a bookcase, and a list of suppliers would soon become out of date. Instead, this chapter shows you some of the major considerations in selecting a system.

You can find an excellent list of suppliers for these systems and services by consulting *Presentations* magazine (Lakewood Publications, www.presentations.com or 800-707-7749). Start with its annual *Buyers Guide to Presentation Products*, which comes as a supplement in the December issue. Other sources include your computer equipment supplier, consultants, and the phone book under Audio-Visual Equipment, Teleconferencing, or Videoconferencing (start with Video in the index of the Business to Business Edition of the Yellow Pages).

You can also consult with experts in your organization and local suppliers to design the specific configuration that best meets your needs.

There are several factors you will need to consider when choosing a videoconference system. The following sections describe your options.

Rent or Buy?

Renting

Renting is best if you have an immediate need, plan only occasional use, or want to evaluate this type of system before purchasing. When you rent, you obtain the expertise and services of the provider's technicians. They will help you plan the transmission logistics, make the connections, and manage the transmission part of your meeting.

Most major hotels and some resorts (such as La Casa Del Zorro Desert Resort in Borrego Springs, CA, at 888-336-9336) offer videoconference and teleconference services. You can also rent facilities from phone companies and companies that specialize in this service (such as Affinity at 800-370-7150 or MIVNET at 800-464-8638).

Purchasing

Purchasing a system costs less if you plan frequent use, want full control, or have unique needs. Of course, when you buy a system, you also buy the installation, maintenance, operation, and future renovations for the system. Those costs can exceed the cost of the initial hardware.

Type of System

Room-based

Here, a room is set up specifically for videoconferences. The installation may include monitors (or video projection systems) and speakers. Other equipment includes video cameras, microphones, computers, whiteboards, fax machines, and conference room furniture. Expect to pay $50,000 to over $150,000 for each installation.

➡ **Advantages**

- The entire system, including line connections, major components, and auxiliary equipment, is in place, ready to use.

- You can install a large screen video projection system that displays life-sized images of participants at other locations. This makes it easier for you to see members of other groups and it creates the impression of a more natural meeting than would be possible with a television monitor.

  Some rooms have been set up with the screen and cameras positioned to display life-sized images of the other participants on the other side of the conference table, thus creating the impression of a regular meeting.

- The participants at each location benefit from the same interaction locally that would occur in a regular meeting (compared to meetings conducted by individuals sitting in their offices using desktop systems).

- A formal, first class conference room conveys success, which may be important when meeting with top executives in other companies.

- The cost of a single installation may be less than the total cost of many mobile, remote, or desktop systems.

➡ Disadvantages
- A room-based system costs more than a single mobile system.

- Installed equipment will lack flexibility and be more difficult to replace.

Roll-about

This is a cart-mounted system that can be moved from meeting room to meeting room. Some organizations use a cart-mounted system for a room-based videoconference room.

These systems contain everything needed for a videoconference mounted on a cart: one or two monitors, camera (often mounted above the monitor), sound system, and computer. Expect to pay $10,000 to $60,000 for each system.

➡ Advantages
- Since this system can be moved, almost any

room can serve as a videoconference room. This provides added flexibility by allowing you to use existing conference rooms.

- This is an economical way to support videoconferences. The equipment is generally less expensive and you avoid the renovation required for a room-based system.

- Since these systems are sold as a package, they can be easier to operate.

➥ Disadvantages
- These systems will work only in rooms outfitted with appropriate transmission lines. Thus, obtaining full flexibility may require installing an expensive communications system throughout the entire facility. Of course, if your company already has such a system in place (for example, to support a computer network), then it is simply a matter of providing the appropriate connections in conference rooms.

- The system must be connected each time it is moved.

- A sophisticated system with two monitors will be a large piece of equipment (imagine two refrigerators tied together) that is difficult to move about.

- TV monitors project smaller images than video projection systems.

Desktop
The participants sit at their desks and use their personal computers or workstations. Since these computers already have a monitor and (generally) a loudspeaker, only a video camera, microphone, and software are needed. Expect to pay about $1,000 for each system. Realize that the total expenditure for this approach equals the cost for one system multiplied by the number of systems. If your organization is sufficiently large, that can exceed the cost of a room-based system.

➥ Advantages

- They use equipment, such as a desktop computer, that may be already in place.

- These are much less expensive for a single installation.

- They use transmission lines that are already in place, such as the Internet or the company's intranet.

- They are generally the easiest systems to set up and operate. Depending upon the computer, you may need to provide only software.

- The members of the organization assume responsibility for scheduling their meetings. That eliminates the need to work with the technicians and support staff that maintain room-based systems. This promotes teamwork and productivity.

- They make is easy to hold informal meetings.

- Participants meet while sitting at their desks, thus eliminating all travel time.

- These systems are appropriate for videoconferences (or video telephone calls between small groups).

- Some of these systems also support collaborative efforts on developing computer files.

➤ **Disadvantages**

- The total cost to purchase and install a large number of systems can be very high.

- The video appears as a small (e.g., 2-in. by 1.5-in.), poor quality image on a computer screen (instead of a full-screen picture on a large monitor or projection screen). Thus, these systems are acceptable for informal meetings between small groups. You can expect a maximum transmission rate of about 10 frames per second (fps) for point-to-point (two people) meetings. The frame rate will decrease to less than one fps as more images are displayed. That means that with eight people, you may be watching snap shots that change every few of seconds.

- The apparent simplicity of holding such meetings can lure people into neglecting the planning and discipline that makes them productive.

Frame Rate

The frame rate is the number of video frames displayed each second on the monitors. Broadcast quality occurs at 30 frames per second (fps) and requires high quality (expensive) transmission systems. Ten fps is considered the minimum frame rate for acceptable video quality.

Low frame rates appear jerky to viewers. That can affect the quality of your meeting if it distracts participants or creates a poor impression of your organization. When selecting a system, be sure to evaluate the impact of frame rate on a prospective system's image quality.

Some simple systems will deliver very slow frame rates. For example, if you use a desktop system on the Internet with a 28.8 kps (thousand bits per second) modem connected to a standard phone line, you will experience noticeable waits while each frame draws on your screen. You can improve the speed by displaying fewer video windows or (sometimes) selecting a smaller video window (like a postage stamp).

Sound

Most videoconference systems send the audio signal with the video. If the video is slow, you may also obtain poor quality (choppy) audio. This makes a bad impression on viewers. One video expert reports that bad audio degrades apparent video quality. Some video systems attempt to balance the quality of video and audio reception.

Some simple systems (such as desktop systems) rely on the telephone to convey the audio signal, which produces acceptable sound.

In a teleconference, you will need microphones and speakers. If you have a large room, you may need additional speakers and microphones so that everyone can hear everyone else.

Transmission Systems

The following transmission systems provide widely different levels of video quality. Conventional meetings within an organization may find a single ISDN line to be acceptable. Meetings with top executives in other companies will probably necessitate transmissions with multiple ISDN lines or a T-1 line. Broadcast meetings demanding high quality video and flexibility will most likely be handled by satellite. Desktop systems may be served with intranet or Internet connections.

➡ Standard Phone Line
This is barely adequate for desktop systems. Video will be choppy and limited to small images.

➡ ISDN Phone Line
These high speed phone lines allow transmission of up to 128 thousand bits per second (kps) per

line, which provides a maximum of 15 fps of
video. When three ISDN lines are combined, up
to 384 (kps) of information can be sent, producing
30 fps. Note that a system claiming to operate at
30 fps may actually deliver less, such as 27 fps,
depending upon system capabilities and line
traffic.

➡ T-1

This high speed digital line can transmit data,
voice with graphics, and video. A T-1 line operates at 1,540 kps and will support 30 fps. As you
might expect, a T-1 line is expensive to install and
operate.

➡ Cable TV

Some cable TV companies are offering a new
service that connects home-based desktop systems to the Internet through their networks. This
is a high speed (1,540 kps or more) line that
provides home offices with a T-1 quality transmission. The effective transmission speeds depend upon the Internet servers, Internet traffic
loads, and desktop computer speeds to transfer
and process information.

➡ Satellite TV

Some satellite TV systems can connect computers
to the Internet through their satellite TV networks. Currently, this requires a special dish.
Transmission speeds are at least as high as what

is available from cable TV.

➡ Satellite

This produces the best broadcast quality video with the greatest flexibility. You can set up a site whereever you can erect a satellite dish (sizes range from 0.9 to 1.8 meters diameter). Such a station is referred to as a *very small aperture terminal* (VSAT). It is also the most expensive.

➡ Intranet

This is the computer network installed within your company. Its operation depends upon the capabilities of the server (computer that manages the system) and the transmission system.

➡ Internet

Video quality will depend upon how your system is connected to the Internet. If you are using modems connected to standard phone lines, the frame rate will be very slow. If you are connected by a T-1 line, you can receive fast (broadcast quality) frame rates. Actual speeds will depend upon servers, Internet traffic, and the computers that you use.

Other Equipment

➡ Video Monitors

A monitor is simply a TV or the video screen with

a personal computer. A larger screen is easier to
see and more expensive. Expect to pay from
hundreds to thousands of dollars. You can obtain
these from a video or computer retailer.

➡ Video Projection Systems
Video projection systems provide large displays
through a variety of systems (LCD projector,
video projector). These can create life-sized
images in videoconferences or giant images in
theaters to address large audiences. Expect to pay
$3,000 to $15,000, or even more.

➡ Video Camera
The range of possibilities is huge, from simple
black and white cameras that mount on a
computer's monitor (costing less than $100) to
high quality digital cameras costing over $7,500.

Cameras can be mounted on a monitor, placed on
a tripod, controlled by a sound activation system
that aims the camera at the person speaking,
controlled remotely by a conference director, or
operated by a photographer.

You can obtain these from a video retailer or
purchase them with the video system.

➡ Microphones
These can be built into the video camera, set on
tables (one for each participant or a single
speakerphone unit), worn on clothing, or built

into the conference table. Although you would most likely obtain these with the video system, you can also purchase them from an audio equipment retailer.

➥ Computers

Most remote meetings benefit from having a computer available. With audioconferences, it can provide a running list of ideas in a chat session over the Internet. It also allows the participant to calculate possibilities, develop text, or browse through information resources. Obtain these from your computer retailer.

➥ Whiteboard

This is an electronic chalkboard. Different models will either print copies of the information written on the board (copyboards), save information as computer files (peripheral whiteboards), or allow interactive writing on the board (interactive whiteboards). This last type of system uses computers to manage the displays and digital projection to show images. These can support audio and videoconferences by letting you send the information written on the board to the other locations.

➥ Bridge (Multipoint Conferencing Server)

This is a sophisticated communications device that serves as a video traffic controller.

A bridge provides two functions.

- The bridge routes multipoint (more than two) video and audio signals to different sites. Video can be displayed in one of four (split screen) windows displayed simultaneously or controlled by a variety of selection schemes. In the latter case, someone chooses the site that is to act as the broadcast site, sending its signal to the other sites.

- The bridge converts transmission protocols used by different systems into either a standard protocol or into protocols understood by the receiving systems.

Thus, you will need a bridge for:

- Conferences among three or more locations

- Conferences between two systems transmitting different protocols (described below)

If you hold few multipoint meetings, you will most likely rent bridge services. Your transmission or facility provider should be able to direct you to appropriate sources.

It is probably most cost effective to purchase a bridge if your company has installed videoconference systems at more than 40 locations and holds frequent multipoint meetings. Expect to pay at least $150,000 per unit.

➡ Transmission Protocols

Some companies have developed proprietary protocols for the video signals handled by their systems. This allows them to optimize system performance by assembling a video signal that takes advantage of their hardware design. Without a bridge, these systems can communicate only with systems using the same protocol.

To resolve this, most newer systems offer a variety of protocol options. These may include the manufacturer's proprietary protocol, other proprietary protocols, and the standard protocol (H.320).

The general types of bridge transmission (or translation) services are:

Proprietary. The bridge routes signals between systems with identical protocols. This provides the highest quality signal, since it has been optimized for the system's hardware.

Standard. All systems use the standard protocol (H.320). This produces a generally lower quality reception because the standard protocol is a signal that has been designed to work with all systems (no optimization).

Analog. The bridge translates the protocol from the sending system to the protocol understood by the receiving systems. It does this by translating one proprietary protocol to an analog signal, which is later translated to the other system's proprietary protocol.

Key Ideas

- Choose equipment that best serves the types of meetings that you hold most often. In some organizations, simple desktop systems set up for key individuals may suffice. Other organizations may require sophisticated installations of high-end systems.

- Consider total system cost when evaluating the system. An inexpensive desktop system installed in hundreds of offices can cost more than a fixed installation.

- Begin by renting the service from a variety of providers to gain experience in capabilities and equipment options.

Chapter 14

Computer-Aided Meetings

What They Are

Computers can dramatically increase the efficiency and effectiveness of meetings. They can help a group quickly gather ideas, record progress, process results, and display information. The possibilities are widely varied, depending upon the type of system used.

You can use computers to conduct the following types of meetings.

➡ Standard Meetings

A group of four to twelve people holds a "standard" meeting with computers. For most of the meeting, the computers serve as an enhanced chart pad. Each person types ideas or responses into a laptop computer, which is linked to a main computer that manages the activity. Later, the participants sort, prioritize, and vote for ideas. Progress is fast-paced, focused, and dynamic.

Generally, there is one computer for each participant. Laptop computers are most commonly used because they occupy less space, allow the participants to see one another easily, avoid a permanent installation, and provide mobility to participants at other locations.

The facilitator manages the meeting activities through a central computer that gathers, stores, and displays information. The software (groupware) that manages such meetings offers a variety of capabilities. For example, it can:

- Provide a structure for collecting ideas, votes, and other information

- Collect and tally information such as votes, answers to surveys, and other data either publicly or anonymously

- Display ideas, decisions, and outcomes on a central computer screen, large monitor, or projection screen

- Calculate statistics related to votes, surveys, and prioritizations

- Display results in a variety of formats, such as tables, bar charts, and graphs

- Allow the participants to send messages to each other or to the facilitator during the meeting

- Make word processors, spreadsheets, and other software tools available to the participants

- Allow the participants to collaborate on the same file (text document, spreadsheet, etc.) with software tools

- Record and save action items, decisions, and other results produced during the meeting

➡ Survey Meetings

A facilitator poses questions to a group that could include hundreds of participants. Each participant votes for answers on a digital keypad or on a standard keyboard (less common). The keypads send their responses either by wire or by radio signal to a receiver that is connected to a main computer.

The facilitator has prepared for this meeting by loading questions with multiple choice or numerical answers into the main computer. This system helps the facilitator conduct dynamic surveys coupled with immediate evaluations and responses to the results.

The software managing such a meeting collects the responses and processes them into bar charts, plots, and statistics. Some systems also display an indicator during voting (such as a moving bar) that shows the fraction of votes collected. The software uses only the most recent response from each keypad for its calculations. This allows people to change their votes and also prevents multiple votes from distorting results.

➡ Collaborative Work Meetings

Participants work jointly on the same computer file (such as a text document, spreadsheet, page layout, illustration, or software code).

Although this type of meeting can be held with any size group, it is generally most effective (and manageable) with small groups of two to six. Such a meeting can be held with all the participants in one room or with each participant at a different location. Most commonly the participants sit in their offices and use the computers on their desks.

These systems allow people to collaborate with:

- Text interaction. The participants work on the same computer file, which is displayed on each person's screen. A participant's initials will appear on the cursor when that person is making changes or each participant will have a separate cursor. Participants communicate by typing messages that appear in a chat window on each computer screen.

- Voice interaction. The software may transmit voice through your intranet or the Internet. The participants may also speak by means of a standard telephone conference call.

- Voice and video interaction. The software may transmit voice and video through your intranet or the Internet.

- Combinations. The software may transmit text, voice, or video. The participants also may use this software with other audio- or video conference systems.

Applications

The following scenarios show how computers can increase the productivity or improve the efficiency of meetings.

➡ A New Design

A marketing team of eight people met to design an advertisement for a new product. By holding a computer-aided meeting, they greatly improved their effectiveness on this project.

First, they conducted a brainstorm session to invent a new name for the product. While the participants typed ideas into their computers, the main computer collected and displayed all the ideas in a master list shown on the projection screen.

The facilitator prodded the team with thought-provoking questions, such as, "What would this product name itself? Suppose the product's parents came from Iceland? What's your last idea inside-out?"

At the end of three minutes, the brainstorm session was stopped so the group could rest.

They spent two minutes watching a slide show of award-winning advertisements that were displayed on the main screen. This served to stir their creative thinking by showing other design possibilities.

Meanwhile the facilitator sorted the list of ideas (using the central computer) to eliminate duplicates. Then the brainstorming resumed.

At the end of another three minutes, the group had collected a total of 107 unique ideas.

Next, the participants voted for the most memorable names with their computers. Each time they voted, the computer displayed a mark next to the choice and recorded the number of choices remaining. The vote produced four names with unanimous support; the group then voted again to prioritize them.

This entire process took about fifteen minutes.

Then the team wrote drafts of advertisements. They divided the task into four parts, which they assigned to pairs of team members. Each pair worked together on the same word processor file, drafting the text.

At the end of 20 minutes, the pairs took turns showing their drafts to the rest of the team. Everyone offered suggestions that made the text more compelling, while the facilitator typed these revisions on the master computer. Sometimes the ideas flowed so fast that the facilitator had to ask the group to save their ideas on their personal copies of the draft.

At the end of an hour, the team had completed drafts of four advertisements. The next step was to present the drafts to their management at the corporate office. Of course, they plan to meet through a videoconference.

➡ Feedback for Management

The president of a software firm wanted to deal with rumors that started after the company's stock dropped from 29 to 15 dollars per share. Apparently, a vocal group of employees had been blaming management for poor planning and bad leadership. This, in turn, was affecting morale and productivity.

To address the charges, the president decided to hold a meeting with all 150 employees, supported by a computerized survey system. Multiple choice questions would be displayed by an LCD projector on a large screen and the employees would use numerical key pads to vote for answers. The computer would collect votes, process data, and display results on the screen.

Some of the questions and their answers were:

- I own company stock. (Yes, No)
- The stock will return to $29 a share by the end of the year (Five choices from 1 = Strongly Agree to 5 = Strongly Disagree)

- What had the most impact on the drop in stock price?

  1. Management

  2. Changes in the stock market

  3. A 5% drop in earnings last quarter

  4. A second-place rating by a major trade journal of our software

The president opened the meeting by telling the employees that management valued their help in making the business successful. The company faced a crisis and it was essential that everyone work together.

During the meeting, the facilitator introduced each question and explained the choices for the answers. Based on suggestions from the employees, the list of answers was revised for two of the questions and a new question was added to the survey.

After each survey response was displayed, the president commented on its implications and invited questions from the employees. In general, the survey system set the stage for candid discussions of critical issues related to the company's future.

After the meeting, the president admitted that some of the responses were a surprise. This proved valuable because that information helped management make changes to improve the business. Other responses seemed to surprise the employees, which also proved valuable. Many employees made changes in their work as a result of the meeting. And best of all, the rumors stopped.

Benefits

Computers enhance work capability in the following ways:

- Computers allow everyone to contribute ideas at the same time. That lets you collect and process information more quickly than if you have to wait for a scribe to write each idea on a chart pad.

- Computers let people see the results of their work immediately. For example, the results of surveys can be displayed as charts, increasing their comprehension and impact.

- Collaborative efforts to develop computer files makes full use of teamwork. Documents, budgets, software, illustrations, layouts, schematics, and schedules can be developed faster with the combined wisdom of a team.

- Computers keep people focused. The work pace is so rapid that it becomes impossible to become distracted. Also, people generally pay attention to computer screens and television monitors.

- The system saves a record of everything produced during the meeting. That helps you prepare accurate minutes, save valuable information, or resume the meeting after a break.

- People learn how to use most groupware quickly.

Special Considerations

When planning computer meetings, you may have to deal with the following disadvantages:

- These systems can be complex and expensive. Technicians may be needed to set up, operate, and maintain the equipment and software.

- If a component fails, the meeting ends or has to continue with conventional procedures.

- Some features of these systems offer new opportunities to misbehave. For example, secondary conversations can take place through messages sent silently between participants, or participants can ignore the facilitator during a survey meeting while they read information on the screen.

- It is possible for tools to become toys. Make sure people make appropriate use of computers to increase productivity.

- Extensive instruction may be necessary to use the system fully.

- If the computers remove rather than enhance human interaction, the participants may conclude that the meeting lacked fair process.

What to Do

In general, the way you conduct these meetings will depend upon the capabilities of your system. The following suggestions should apply in all cases:

- As with any meeting, adequate planning leads to success. Prepare an agenda that makes optimum use of the capabilities of your system. Identify in your agenda when and how the computers will be used.

- Check to see if the use of computers enhances the meeting process. If the meeting can be conducted without computer-assisted idea collection or data analysis, consider holding the meeting in a conventional conference room. You want to avoid renting a truck to carry a pencil.

- If appropriate, meet with the technicians before the meeting to load files related to your issues, enter survey options, and plan statistical analyses.

- You (or your assistant) should also arrive early to make sure that everything in the system works.

- Set up and agree upon ground rules before the meeting.

- Include a facilitator or system operator. This is more important for a computer-assisted meeting than for other types of meetings because operating the system can be a full-time job. If you attempt to do it, you will attend your meeting as a technician instead of as a participant.

- Define a culture for issues such as interacting with the system, asking for assistance, and dealing with unproductive activities.

- If your system is complex (one company sent its employees to a one-week seminar to learn how to use their new system) make sure everyone has been fully instructed on using the system before the meeting. Unskilled participants become weak links in the process that can undo any advantages of using advanced technology. You want to spend your time holding a meeting instead of conducting a class.

- During the meeting, make sure there is an appropriate amount of human interaction. This, after all, is the reason why you called a meeting.

- Check calculated results with quick estimates and ask the participants if they agree with outcomes. You want to avoid being fooled by results that reflect technical quirks instead of consensus.

Key Ideas

- Computers provide sophisticated tools for displaying information, collecting ideas, and analyzing results.

- Make sure these tools enhance instead of embellish your meeting.

- Extensive planning and preparation are needed to use these tools fully.

- Make sure the meeting includes enough human interaction so everyone feels that it represented a fair process.

Chapter 15

Yes, You Can!

A Final Thought

You can hold effective meetings with any group. The keys are:

Focus everyone's thinking on producing results by using structured process tools.

Introduce every issue as a question.

Plan agendas like budgets where you spend resources in proportion to the value of the expected results.

Honor the participants by stating positive expectations and recording their ideas.

Maintain a safe environment by modeling and requesting cooperative participation.

Work as a team to achieve results that lead to common gain for your organization.

I wish you the best of success as you use these techniques for your effective meetings.

Suggested Reading

Mastering Meetings
The 3M Meeting Management Team, with
 Jeannine Drew

People Skills
Robert Bolton

Discover Desktop Conferencing With Netmeeting 2.0
Mike Britton and Suzanne Van Cleve

Effective Meetings: The Complete Guide
Clyde W. Burleson

How to Make Meetings Work
Michael Doyle

How to Run a Successful Meeting in Half the Time
Milo O. Frank

Listening Your Way to Management Success
Allan Glatthorn and Herbert Adams

The Art of Facilitation: How to Create Group Synergy
Dale Hunter, Anne Bailey, Bill Taylor

117 Tips for Effective Meetings
Steve Kaye

Meetings in an Hour or Less
Steve Kaye

Influencing With Integrity
Genie Laborde

Smart Questions
Dorothy Leeds

We've Got to Start Meeting Like This: A Guide to Successful Business Meetings Management
Roger K. Mosvick and Robert B. Nelson

The Lost Art of Listening
Michael P. Nichols

Robert's Rules of Order
Henry M. Robert

Enhanced Cu-SeeMe
Robert Rustici

Official Microsoft NetMeeting 2.0 Book
Robert Summers

Power Talking: 50 Ways to Say What You Mean and Get What You Want
George Walther

Index

About Steve Kaye, Ph.D.

Steve Kaye can help you increase productivity, master priorities, and find solutions. As a consultant, author, and professional speaker, he shows people how to achieve success.

Steve has a Ph.D. in chemical engineering from Carnegie Mellon University and 20 years of experience working for major corporations.

He is also the author of:

Meetings in an Hour or Less

117 Tips for Effective Meetings

His workshops and presentations inform, inspire, and entertain.

Want to know more? Call today for info.

Steve Kaye
P.O. Box 208
Placentia, CA 92871-0208
Phone: 714-528-1300 • 888-421-1300
FAX: 714-528-2123 • 888-421-2123

Or visit his web site for articles, program details, and background information.

http://www.stevekaye.com